getting it all together

Roy C. Putnam

ABINGDON • Nashville

GETTING IT ALL TOGETHER

Copyright © 1977 by Abingdon

Library of Congress Cataloging in Publication Data

PUTNAM, ROY C 1928-
    Getting it all together.
    1. Bible. N.T. Ephesians—Criticism, interpretation, etc. I. Title.
BS2695.2.P87   227'.5'06   76-28456

ISBN 0-687-14114-1

Text on p. 84 is taken from *The East, No Exit* by Os Guinness. © 1974 by Inter-Varsity Christian Fellowship and used by permission of InterVarsity Press.

Text on p. 27 is from *Trousered Apes*. Copyright © 1971 by Churchill Press Limited. All rights reserved. Published in the United States by Arlington House, Inc., New Rochelle, New York.

Foreword copyright © 1972 by Arlington House, Inc. All rights reserved.

Text on p. 12 is from *God's Order* by John A. Mackay. Copyright 1953 by Macmillan Publishing Co., Inc.

Text on p. 42 is from Geoffrey King's *Truth for Our Time*. Used by permission of Eerdmans Publishing Co.

Scripture quotations noted RSV are from the Revised Standard Version of the Bible, copyrighted 1946, 1952, © 1971, 1973.

Scripture quotation noted NEB is from The New English Bible. © the Delegates of the Oxford University Press and the Syndics of the Cambridge University Press 1961, 1970. Reprinted by permission.

Scripture quotation noted TLB is from *The Living Bible*, copyright © 1971 Tyndale House Publishers, Wheaton, Illinois. Used by permission.

MANUFACTURED BY THE PARTHENON PRESS AT
NASHVILLE, TENNESSEE, UNITED STATES OF AMERICA

To the
congregation
of
Trinity United Methodist Church
whose warm receptivity
and heightened expectancy
toward the preached Word
gladden the heart and quicken the mind
of its preacher
this volume
is
gratefully dedicated

That in the dispensation of the fulness of times he might gather together in one all things in Christ, both which are in heaven, and which are on earth; even in him.

Ephesians 1:10

Contents

Acknowledgments

The specific stimulus for the preparation of this book comes from audiences who have gained knowledge of the contents in verbal form. Lectures were first given before the Good News Convocation at Lake Junaluska, North Carolina, and then at other Bible conferences. Requests came subsequently for their inscription.

Since the larger context into which these words have been spoken represents denominational and cultural heterogeneity, I have assumed that these pages would appeal to the straits of the souls of all who are questing for the endless glories that shine from the sacred page.

These words are now subjected to the discipline of manuscript composition. I trust that the syntax, etymology, and rubric through which they pass will not dull their cutting edge. Evangelicals, with whom I most enthusiastically identify, are no different in this wise—we, too, need a departure from banal repetition of halting, colorless expressions of what the Bible has already said more effectively in its own unconcealable way.

A New Zealand friend reminded me that God sometimes blesses even "a poor exegesis of a bad translation of a doubtful reading of an obscure verse of a minor prophet." I surely belong to the category of the minor prophet. But my intent is for a book with enough provocative stabs to send the imagination spinning into new corners of unexplored truth. May the Holy Spirit be pleased to drive the truth with his own compelling force.

Constraint is upon me to acknowledge with deep gratitude those who have helped me "get it all together" in book form.

To my dear wife, Flada, who has passed these sentences through both "ear-gate" and "eye-gate" and who has with a perceptive critique assisted me in refining the propositions. Mention must also be made of our faithful secretary, Kris Hackman, who with poise and grace has typed the manuscript in its various stages. But above all, praise unto him who "inspires the living faith which whosoe'er receives, the witness in himself he hath and consciously believes."

INTRODUCTION

Getting it all together is what the old Adamic Improvement Society cannot do. But it is what Christ has done and will yet do in and through his church.

Discord and division and death stalk the world. Conflict and doubt batter and besiege the church. This slashes into our unity, breaking concentration and deflecting energies. As we view the modern scene we reflect a world that is fractured and fragmented, rifled and rifted and restive, nihilistic in purpose, and morally vacuous.

The modern analyst assesses this world's present absurdity and asks "Why?" The spiritually enlightened evangelical Christian assesses this world's powerful potential and asks "Why not?" And, mind you, this is not some optimistic humanism in which we are engaging. This is revealed theology. The eyes of our understanding have been opened by the Holy Spirit and by the Word of God to see the hope of Christ's calling.

Through all the murky darkness of sin's vast empire, the Christian sees a throne, "a glorious high throne from the beginning is the place of our sanctuary" (Jer. 17:12). That throne is immutable. "Yet have I set my King upon my holy hill of Zion. Ask of me, and I shall give thee [Christ] the heathen [nations] for thine inheritance, and the uttermost parts of the earth for thy possession" (Ps. 2:6, 8).

God has set a purpose for himself. That purpose is to bring all that is in the universe into the unity of Christ and under his benevolent reign (Eph. 1:10). This means that all the conflicting loyalties of men and nations are being gathered up and centered in Christ Jesus. What an astounding thought! And it is more breathtaking when we recall what this implies. For the disunity that sin wrought in the historic fall of man struck in four directions or dimensions. It struck: (1) upward to the throne of God; (2) inward to the human spirit; (3) downward to the material creation; and (4) onward through the historical process.

The unity that Christ proposes, promises, and assures affects all these dimensions, establishing oneness between man and God, man and his true self, man and his fellows, and man and his environment. Nothing less than total redemption!

What God is able to project he is also able to actualize. What assurance have we of this? We have it demonstrated and measured and attested to by the power that raised Jesus from the dead. The surging soul of the great apostle strains at the leash of language to exhaust the vocabulary of power in describing this in Ephesians 1:19-23. Death itself cannot deter God's forward movement in history and beyond.

But what is more exciting is this: the power that raised Jesus Christ from the dead is available to his church. This is not some diffused energy. It is directive power. Indeed it is "to us-ward who believe" (Eph. 1:19). That is Paul's statement in the reliable, archaic King James language. The image is that of a power zeroed in on us. The church becomes the focal point in history and the chosen instrument of God in setting forth an object lesson of this unity.

So the theme of this book concerns itself with the *message* and *methods* of the church, to be sure. But the theme also concerns itself with the *mood* and *manner* and *motivation* of the church. The Christian, then, bathed in the light of Holy Spirit wisdom and revelation, is enabled to bring "thrones and dominions, principalities and powers" within the sweep of his vision. A part of this insight was held by the little girl in Carl Sandburg's poem who said, "Someday they are going to have a war and nobody is coming." This is the vision that beholds death as it mounts the scaffold and becomes the museum piece of the ages. This is the dream that sees the dawn of that day of triumph, "not then, but now; not there but here," and shouts to the unborn generations, "Now unto him that is able to do exceeding abundantly above all that we ask or think, according to the power that worketh in us, unto him be glory in the church by Christ Jesus throughout all ages, world without end. Amen" (Eph. 3:20-21).

The Hope of His Calling

An appropriate subtitle of Ephesians might be: The High Calling of God, or The Hope of His Calling. It is my conviction that the church today needs, more than anything else, not a new efficiency but a new "Ephesianscy," a new concept, if you please, a new sense of the calling of God—something to enhance us, to elevate us, to envision us, and to energize us. If we allow the impulse of this call of God to stir within us, and the concept of this call to master our thinking, then God will again clothe his divine activity in our failing flesh and breathe his sanctity through the heat of our desire. Then the church will march under a fresh anointing and a full mandate, fair as the moon, bright as the sun, and glorious as an army with banners.

Ephesians could be commended with many words. Samuel Taylor Coleridge called it the most divine composition of man. But a more discerning theological tribute has been paid this New Testament book by Dr. John Mackay, president emeritus of Princeton Theological Seminary. He suggests that Ephesians is "the most contemporary book in the Bible," for three reasons. First, "it proclaims the essential image." Second, it presents the true basis for the communal life of mankind. And third, it provides for us life with a lilt.

Essential Image

Our first reflections focus on the essential image. We all realize that man has abandoned the original image and has become himself an image-maker and image-creator.

A group of soldiers returned late from a Saturday night spree, and then very languidly made their way to the chapel services on Sunday morning. The chaplain spoke on the Ten

Commandments, and one of the soldiers was heard to remark as he left the service, "Well, at least I haven't made any graven images."

But I wonder. Have you talked with Mr. Average Church Member lately about his ideas of the Bible, God, or eternity? The average man holds in his mind a concept of God that is quite alien to the Scriptures. That concept has nothing to do with the God who is Father of our Lord Jesus Christ. As a matter of fact, the more people talk to me about their ideas of God, the more I am convinced that their God exists only in their imaginations.

When I am asked to exchange the thoughts and concepts of the Bible for some contemporary thinking such as God's existing as "the ground of being," I see no advance on the idea of God as Father of our Lord Jesus Christ, the Lord of heaven and earth. I'm reminded of the drunk who complained, "All day long I keep asking the time, and all day long, people keep giving me different answers."

I like the definitions of our Christian faith that we find in the Scriptures. God is defined in terms of Jesus Christ.

When Simeon held this little Child in his arms in the temple, he said, "This child is set for the fall and rising again of many in Israel" (Luke 2:34). This child is set. That is, everything is predestined in terms of Jesus Christ.

An outstanding missionary evangel, whose life was invested in India, interpreted Christ to the Hindu culture by saying, "Jesus Christ is not only written into the text, he is written into the texture of things. Not only written in the Bible, but written into biology."

This means for the Christian that Jesus Christ is the source, center, and sanction of all life. When we talk of *Christus Victor*, "Christ victorious through the cross and resurrection," it is not just a pious hope, it is an irrevocable fact!

Our gospel is not something that is superimposed on mankind. The will of God fits man, because man was made for it. Jesus said, "My yoke is easy." Any other yoke is hard,

13

because it doesn't fit. "My meat" said Jesus, "is to do the will of him that sent me." The will of God was his food, his strength. It nourished and sustained him. Life is fulfilled in terms of Jesus Christ. That is why we say that he is not an imposition on life. He is the exposer of life, revealing the heart of reality as the true nature of man, of God, of the universe. When we live out our lives in the will of God, life *sings*. Go against that will and life *sighs*.

This is because Jesus is the essential image of the universe. He is reality, not simply written on the pages of an archaic book. He is plowed into the very furrows of the nature of life itself.

Without Christ we cannot define life, sin, death, immortality, or anything else. Sin only shows up as exceedingly sinful when Jesus comes. He exposes the malevolent heart of evil which would crucify incarnate love. Truth has no meaning apart from him. What is truth? What is reality? What is right? Without reference to God incarnate in Jesus Christ we would live in the hell of an illusory world.

Today many have lost their grip on reality, because they have lost their contact with Christ. The world has become for them an illusion. It is Jesus who exposes something true at the very core of existence, something reliable, something real. In architecture, for example, we rely on something true. We drop a plumb line to decide whether a wall is straight or crooked. That plumb line exposes the trueness of the wall. Jesus is God's plumb line. The same applies to art, music, literature. In music we sound the universal note A, thus tuning our musical instruments with precision. Jesus is God's true note.

Christ is the essential image. Everything is predestined in terms of him. This is the reason the Christian faith begins with what God has already done in raising Christ from the dead and in setting him at the Father's right hand, far above all principalities and powers and mights and dominions and every name.

When we understand our gospel, we know that it is more than an exhortation to *do* this or *be* that. When I was growing up, swinging my legs under a church pew, I was listening to the voice of the pulpit. Perhaps I was obtuse. The broadcast may have been clear, but my receiver was very inadequate. This is what I thought I was getting: "You can and you must!" And I couldn't and I didn't! The message coming through to me was to the effect that if I disciplined myself, aspired to higher goals, followed the gleam (I never learned what the gleam was), then, eventually, when I died, I would get to heaven.

To me, heaven was synonymous with that kind of Sunday preaching. I thought that going to heaven would mean sitting on some damp cloud and plucking an ectoplasmic harp while I was preached to, through all eternity. I was like the little girl that Brother Rufus Mosely used to talk about. She said she wouldn't mind going to heaven if only she could go down to the other place and play with the children on Saturday afternoon.

But the real point of the gospel is the proclamation of what God has already done. God has *already* blessed us, Paul says in Ephesians 1:30, *already* lifted us into the heavenlies in Christ Jesus. Therefore, we are to walk on earth worthy of the vocation into which we have been called.

In the opening three chapters of Ephesians, Paul gives us our definitive theology about the church. Without this, truth can be revised to suit the concensus of the community.

We cannot worship acceptably without knowledge of the One whom we seek to worship. And that personal knowledge of God is our creed, whether or not it be formalized. Faith is not some cognitive wand that we wave; faith is a solid, historical resting place. When we say (that God is) Father of our Lord Jesus Christ, then we have brought our gospel down to history. That's the reason Paul says we are to hold fast to our confession of faith.

We are to come boldly to the throne of grace, but we

cannot do this until we first of all hold to our confession. If we are going to hold to something, it must be substantive. (One can't harpoon a jellyfish or nail whipped cream to a barn door.) We must get hold of the truth that is defined in Scripture.

The gospel is the good news of what God has done; telling men to come to Christ is not good news. Coming to Christ is the necessary implication of the gospel, but to proclaim Christ is to create the faith which precipitates the crisis of response.

God has set a purpose for himself that has been defined for us in terms of Jesus Christ. In the opening chapter of Ephesians, Paul says that all life is predestined to be interpreted in terms of God's Son. When I speak the word *predestination*, I'm treading ground that has been strewn with the scalps of many theological gladiators. I used to read the words *predestination* and *election*, then cough, and go on to the next verse. I imagined that another segment of the church could handle that, so I would leave it.

Yet this doctrine has become for me the substance, the solace upon which I pillow my head at night and to which I awaken in every new dawn, knowing that my steps are ordered of the Lord and that I'm not the doomed plaything of accident and chance and futility.

In this first chapter of Ephesians, Paul is not talking about some arbitrary selection by which a few are chosen to be saved and others are fated to be lost.

A. M. Hunter of Scotland says that *predestination* means, in simple terms, that God chose us before we chose him, that God does not choose us because we deserve it, and that God does not choose us to be his favorites but to be his servants. God did not choose Abraham to be a separatist but to invest him back into the world in order that in him and in his seed "shall all families of the earth be blessed" (Gen. 12:3). "Ye have not chosen me," Jesus said (John 15:16). He meant that you have not chosen me for your purpose, but I have chosen you for my purpose. *Predestination* really means that I'm in business with God to achieve his ends.

This is the reason Paul prays that the eyes of our understanding may be enlightened so that we may know what is the hope of his calling. God's calling is much greater than our understanding of it; our concepts are much too small. C. S. Lewis says the high calling of God is not only beyond our *deserving,* it is often beyond our *desiring,* because we have never been stimulated by getting into the Word of God and seeing there what God has in mind for his people.

Of course, the idea of God's choosing arbitrarily stultifies human responsibility and strangles the gospel; it cuts the nerve of ethical behavior. I know that there is a school of theology that embraces election and predestination in this very narrow concept. Simply stated, *predestination is grace traced to its earliest source.* And its earliest source is the love of God. For he says we were chosen, in him, before the foundation of the world, that we should be holy and without blame before him in love. We are chosen *in* him, because we are loved *by* him, and that means every person is made for the kingdom of God. Every person is chosen. Every fact about us is woven on the loom of God's predestining purpose. We can tangle the threads and tear the fabric of life by self-will, but we are still made for God.

We must never say that a man is a misfit until we find what he is supposed to fit. Jesus taught that we are made to fit the kingdom. The most basic fact about us is not our sinnerhood but our predestination, which is God's design and purpose. To me, original righteousness is more profound than original sin. One man objected some time ago, saying to me, "But, preacher, doesn't Jeremiah teach us that the heart is deceitful above all things and is desperately wicked?"

I said, "Deceitful, yes, that's right. But what is the heart trying to deceive?" The heart is trying to deceive a God who, as Francis Schaeffer notes, is there. He is there! That's the reason the psalmist says, "Whither shall I go from thy spirit? or whither shall I flee from thy presence? If I ascend up into heaven, thou art there: if I make my bed in hell, behold, thou art there" (Ps. 139:7-8).

The devil doesn't run hell; he's a victim when he gets there. The thing that makes hell hell is the fact that we are made for God and are running counter to our predestination. This affronts the holiness of God, and that is why the world is so miserable. Men are going against their true destiny.

Why do all the rebel poets and the existential philosophers and the sick dramatists keep bringing God into their themes? They are desperately attempting to escape God, but they cannot!

A young lady came to our church several years ago. I had not heard from her across the years. Her husband phoned and said, "We must see you immediately."

They sat in my study and I asked about the nature of the problem. She said, "The problem is I need to get up from this study immediately and go to the altar of this sanctuary and give my heart to Jesus Christ."

I was confounded.

She continued, "You see, three or four years ago I sat in this church and God's call came to my life. I left, failing to respond. Subsequently I was married, moved to the West, and I have been rebelling in my own heart against God's will. I have been totally frustrated and futile since that time, and I know that I need to be saved now."

I said, "Well, you can be saved right where you now are, because no place is sacrosanct."

She said, "I know I can, but God called me to that altar, and I must be saved there."

So we went to the altar, and we opened the Word of God and prayed together. She came up with an assurance that Christ had forgiven her and received her in the Beloved and that his call was upon her. That divine calling wouldn't let her go. It wouldn't let her off. And I thank God it wouldn't let her down.

Jesus is our predestination, so we do not have to resign to feeble fatalism as hapless and hopeless victims of outside forces. Too many people believe the script of life has already been written; it needs only to be acted out. Why is it that we see ourselves as prisoners of our genes, of our times, of our environment? Why do we live, fearing that the next blow is going to fall upon us? I recoil when I recall that pessimistic epitaph: "I expected this and here I am."

Jesus wouldn't even acknowledge death; his disciples had to wring it out of him. When he went to Lazarus' tomb they said, "He's dead." But Jesus insisted, "He's asleep." Jesus wouldn't allow death to dominate his thinking; his thoughts were controlled by life. Death could not prevail when the Author of life was presiding. The Scriptures say we have been raised together with him, all things have been put under his feet—principalities, powers, mights, dominions, and every name that is named, not only in this world but in that which is to come. The Father has made Jesus to be the head of all things to his church which is his Body, the fullness of him that fills all in all. God has driven deeply into this life an image which is Jesus Christ.

We live in a time of nihilism. People are desperately trying to make sure of their existence in a world where many gamble on false gods and stake their destiny on speculative theologies and philosophies. The hallmark of our time is agonizing disillusionment with scientism, status, and sex. In the midst of all this, how grand and enticing it is to learn of a destiny written into our natures which can free us from the captivity of the temporal and the seduction of the sensual! Predestined to the adoption of Jesus Christ according to the good pleasure of his will! This is a part of the hope of his calling.

Basis for Communal Life

But there is something else. God's Word presents the basic structure which humanity needs for the true expression of its communal life. For "he is our peace," Paul says in Ephesians 2:14, "who has made us both one, and has broken down the dividing wall of hostility" (RSV). An amazing concept!

I have just been reading the nineteenth chapter of Acts, and I am impressed with the heterogeneity of the Ephesian congregation to which Paul was writing. Here was a group of followers of the Lord who had never heard of the Holy Spirit. Paul came preaching in the Holy Spirit, and when the congregation heard it, they jumped up for joy—and some of them jumped too far. In verses 18 and 19 we see a bunch of anxious Christians. Then there were people from the world of magic, the occult. There were also some heady intellectuals. Paul encountered them in the school of Tyrannus. The church also contained those who had been healed by a handkerchief ministry. Pentecostals were there, ex-idol worshipers, and new babes in Christ.

God took that crowd of diverse people and blended them into a brotherhood and fashioned them into a fellowship. Paul could write to them and say, "I heard of your faith in the Lord Jesus, and love unto all the saints" (Eph. 1:15).

What an achievement! The unity that we are seeking in the world today can only be realized in and through the church of Jesus Christ, nowhere else. The dark incorrigibility of human defiance has been brought to an end in Jesus Christ who gathers all things together unto himself, as he says in Ephesians 1:10. This is God's purpose. This is the consummation of the whole plan of redemption.

But history stands over against this unity. Interference broke out in the heavenlies when the angels kept not their first estate. This rebellion caused an atmosphere of strife, conflict, and disruption. It began in heaven, and its repercussions came down to earth in the first family. Cain murdered Abel, and the whole human race experienced this deceitful current of rebellion cutting its keen and uncoverable way right through human life.

The gospel presents a plan whereby God is able to take all the divergent elements (including the hostile, disruptive ones), gather them up, focus them in himself, and permeate all these divergencies, presiding over them as Lord.

In John 17 we have the *basis* of this unity which is oneness with the Father, the Son, and the Holy Spirit. In Psalm 133:1 we have also the *beauty* of this unity: "Behold, how good and how pleasant it is for brethren to dwell together in unity!" And in Ephesians 4 we have the *bond* of this unity; it is the lordship of Jesus Christ. There are seven unities listed, and right in the center is the Lord. It is on the basis of his lordship and our coming under the control of that lordship that life is brought into unity—no other way.

When we proclaim that Jesus is Lord and get men to bow the knee to him, only then does the church begin to form, and it's a spontaneous thing. We become baptized into one Body and are controlled by one Spirit. We cannot have unity any other way. Attempts to put it together organizationally will always fail. (I have a friend who says, "The ecumenical movement reminds me of a religious hash. I don't eat hash away from home, because I don't know what they put in it. I don't eat hash at home, because I *do* know what's in it.")

I came up in a liberal tradition. All my educational exposure was in that wise. But I was converted at the age of seventeen. Theologically I was destitute; I just didn't know a thing. As a matter of fact, I didn't even suspect anything! But I did know to whom I belonged. And I found myself brought right into the context of evangelical Christianity. A good conversion experience will make a person an evangelical Christian posthaste. When we're baptized into the Body, we then begin to partake of the life, begin to obey the Head, and a new, exciting and ordered life begins. This is unity.

Life with a Lilt

"These early Christians," said Major Ian Thomas, "were utterly committed, divinely unafraid, incorrigibly happy, and always in trouble." Incorrigibly happy! We find them without comfort, friends, money, but never without a song. Thanksgiving and praise were the alternating heartbeats of their lives.

Much of the New Testament is a song. When I come to this sacred volume it bears me along on the wings of song. Even the scripture I memorize is not labor. It sings its way into my heart. Life is made to sing.

The book of Job tells us that on the morning of creation, the sons of God shouted for joy and the stars sang together. It is my conviction that this great universe is like an organ. Every star has its radio frequency perfectly tuned; there are no discordant notes. And the stars are all singing together the praises of God. All life is made to sing; this universe has a musical soul.

I used to wonder why the mosquito was made. I just couldn't see any purpose in it. One day I read that the mosquito's wings beat 35,220 times a minute. That rate of vibration produces the perfect tone needed to stimulate the growth of corn! Scientists have discovered that corn grows twice the normal rate when it is planted in an environment where such a tone is constant. Some scientists are inclined to believe that each plant is responsive to an insect wingbeat. Bananas are now grown with a certain tune played constantly on the plantation to stimulate their growth.

God has made us to be free and spontaneous creatures, to live our lives with a lilt. We can go through this world with a song.

> Thy saints in all this glorious war
> Shall conquer, though they die;
> They see the triumph from afar,
> By faith they bring it nigh.   (From Isaac Watts,
>   "Am I a Soldier of the Cross")

We get into the heavenlies and participate in a victory that has cosmic dimensions. There is no problem that we shall ever have that has not already been met and conquered in Jesus Christ. Everything over our head is under his feet. So let us rejoice!

Him and You

Great *wonders* often turn on little *words*. In the second chapter of Ephesians the words *but God* come as a kind of transition when the apostle passes from what he has been saying in the first three verses to what he is going to say. My proposition is that the whole of the Christian life turns on that phrase—*but God*. I suggest that these words should be on our lips more than any others these days.

We live in a world where Christians face the same problems non-Christians face. We are not afforded preferential treatment. God simply won't split human existence and give us the upper floor.

Everywhere people are discussing the human dilemma; never has this concern been more vocalized than today, especially with the present political stimuli. We are talking about what's wrong. We are looking to the left and to the right. But most of us who have assessed the situation in the light of God's Word know that the answer is not in either the left wing or the right wing, because both wings are on the same old sick bird.

History, from one perspective at least, is a sordid, squalid record of man's inhumanity to man, his insatiable greed, his incurable pugnacity, his devilish sadism, and his suicidal urge to destroy civilization. And the problems keep mounting. We have now reached that impasse that H. G. Wells spoke of as "the mind at the end of its tether."

The problem, on the human dimension, is intractable. But when we have finished listening to the voices of despair and pessimism and when the world has said its last word, then Christians will take up where the worldly wise leave off.

Where other religions and philosophies finish, we begin. For God introduces the only hope of mankind.

It is good for us to recognize that ours is not the first problem that God has ever faced. In the beginning this world was in a very distorted shape. The Scriptures say that all was void and without form. Darkness was upon the face of the deep. "But God!" God stood forth, spoke his Word, "Let there be light," and lo, the lightning shafts of a thousand suns set flaming brilliance in the darkest recesses of infinite gloom. And this world began to take form and revolve around its ethereal circle.

There came a time in the history of mankind when confusion reigned. People worshiped false gods. In Ur of the Chaldees, a man by the name of Abram heard the voice of God, and there was born within him the conviction that God was one and indivisible. He knew with inner certainty that if he would obey the voice of this God, then he would somehow find the hope of his calling. Thus Abram marched out in obedience and as a result put his hand upon subsequent centuries and uplifted them into new zones of light and glory. We could drop whole nations into oblivion today, and it would not make as much difference as dropping that one solitary figure from history.

Go right on through history. Just as the situation became so intensely dark, dismal, and desperate, the historian was able to turn a page and on the top write *But God*.

I believe that *but God* is the only answer to the human dilemma today. I can hear somebody saying, "You're overstating your case. That's pulpit exaggeration. Are you literally saying that the gospel of Jesus Christ is the *only* hope?" I am.

Diagnosis: The Energy Crisis

He is our only hope because he alone understands the real cause of our trouble. The twentieth century has been heralded as the greatest century of progress. Yet a man like

Albert Camus, representing the philosophy of our era, says the only serious philosophical problem in our generation is whether to commit suicide! Problems mount that overwhelm our intellectuals; the ecologists have become the eschatologists of our day.

What is the cause of it all? If we fail in the proper diagnosis, we fail in the cure. We have a lot of diagnosticians offering answers, but they have never found the problem. They say we can cure our troubles if we have enough education, enough medication, enough ventilation (talk it out), and enough sanitation.

Some weeks ago a man told me about the economic situation, but I couldn't understand all the complexities. After he got through, I commented, "I think what you're saying is, if our outgo exceeds our income, our upkeep's going to be our downfall." But one wonders who understands.

Once I heard about an Annapolis graduate who was on his first sea voyage. The skipper asked him to chart the latitude and longitude. The young man made his calculations and then brought them to the skipper who read them and then said in a tone of amusement, "Young man, stand at attention. Remove your hat, and continue in a state of reverence."

The young sailor was somewhat perplexed but obeyed. "If your calculations are correct," the skipper continued, "we are at this very moment in the middle of Westminster Abbey."

My dear friends, the Word of God locates us precisely, much better than does man's fallible calculations. Paul says, but God is the answer to the human dilemma, because you were dead, "and you hath he quickened."

That's the problem: animated corpses circulate in our society, having lost the true content of their humanity, because they have fallen out of moral correspondence with God, the source of life and the source of being.

Man was created to experience true humanity which is

God in him. D. T. Niles said, "The dogness of the dog is in the dog but the man-ness of the man is not in the man." Man is created to have a mind that is God taught, to have a will that is God directed, to have emotions that are God satisfied. But Paul declares that man is in a state of deadness because he has broken fellowship with the living God. Today man is trying terribly hard to be morally adult without being spiritually alive. This constitutes the human dilemma. We are attempting to have a self-sustained ethic, which brings to mind the woman who was asked, "Which is more important, the sun or the moon?" She replied, "Why, the moon is more important. It shines at night when we need it. But the sun shines in the daytime when it's light anyhow."

God says man is dead toward Him. In this state of deadness, man follows the course of this world. Why? Because he is living as if there were no God at all, governed entirely by the thing to do, swept by the currents of the age, whatever seems good to his senses. He thinks he is free, but he is not.

A housewife goes to the grocery store. She reaches for a particular item. Why does she do it? She has been brainwashed by the public media. Her mind is in captivity, not in obedience to Christ but to public opinion. This current is a frightening drift.

"A number of logs floating on the surface of a river may point in apparently random directions. The casual observer might regard them as being directionless pieces of timber. But the penetrating eye discerns that in spite of these divergent directions they are all being borne in one direction by the current" (Duncan Williams, *Trousered Apes*).

Everything not anchored in the heavenlies—the realm of manifest reality where Jesus has taken his resurrected humanity—is going to drift. I care not whether it's a majestic liner or a canoe—unless that anchor passes through the uncertainty of the water and fastens itself onto something solid, the boat is current driven. The writer of Hebrews says we have an anchor that's cast within the veil. This is the realm where Jesus is recognized as Lord.

While people follow the current of this world, what determines this course? Not the proprietors of the newspapers and entertainment media. They are but the dupes and instruments of something far more serious. The real controlling force, Paul says, is the "prince of the power of the air, the spirit that now worketh in the children of disobedience."

Man's will does not operate in a vacuum; it attaches itself to some center of value which dictates the content of the will's decision.

Man is a spirit being who will find identification with some spirit, if not the Holy Spirit, then the spirit of this age, the spirit of the Antichrist who now presides over the darkness of this world, this spiritual wickedness in heavenly (high) places. This means that behind the visible scene the basic issues of life are decided. He, the Evil One, is in control of this medium and the course of this world.

One of the most terrifying things about evil is this: it is not static. It is energy. It is no mere negative quality, the absence of goodness. It is a positive malignancy. It is living, powerful, and vital. Paul spoke of the "powers of darkness," "the prince of the power of the air," "the mystery of iniquity that worketh until now." This energy motivates man's self-seeking, self-trust, self-will, self-pleasing, self-glory, and all the other little hyphenated devils that warp and defoliate and spoil life.

We all once lived in the lust of the flesh, fulfilling the desires of the mind. This describes the egalitarian society we have today, in which everything must be made available at all times to everyone. Failing to be human in the idealistic sense of the word, we lapse into a barbaric animalism. We clothe our defeats in high-sounding phraseology such as "alienation," "cult of the unpleasure," "realism," and so forth. But all this fashionable phraseology cannot conceal the fact that the emperor has no clothes. All of this is the lust of the flesh.

What about the lust of the mind? John calls it the pride of life. People are perfectly affable and absolutely delightful—as long as they are allowed to do whatever they want. So we have the new morality, simply an attempt to rationalize and to allow us to give vent to our animal-like passions. Yet all the while, man is trying to be impressively brilliant, tremendously erudite, persuading himself that it's all right to behave like an animal. He calls lying, "smartness"; adultery, "sex experience"; smut and obscenity parade under the false dignity of "frankness."

Man is spiritually dead; and while in this state he is swept by the currents controlled by satanic forces expressing themselves in the lust of the flesh and the mind.

While this condition prevails man is living under the wrath of God. Wrath is the totality of the divine reaction to sin. Wrath is that essential nature of God that puts the mark of disagreement upon man's sin. Wrath is the "no" of God upon all the perversion, all that's not true, all that's not real.

G. Campbell Morgan once made a supposition that the fires of hell and the fires of heaven might be the same fires; in them the saint would be energized, elevated, blessed, fulfilled, and the sinner would be tormented. The same consuming love would delight the one and distress the other.

What I am sure of is that the wrath of God is not something arbitrary and impulsive like that of a provoked driver when someone crosses him.

Once I was in a meeting in a little country church. I came out of a driveway, while noting a big tractor trailer approaching from a distance. Thinking I had plenty of time, I drove out but instantly heard the horn blowing and sensed the displeasure of the truck driver. We came to a stoplight and pulled up side by side. He rolled down his window and began to vent his wrath.

The stoplight changed, and we went on to the next stoplight. I rolled down my window. He was ready for the fray, but I said, "My dear brother, please forgive me for being so thoughtless as to go out in front of you like that. I do trust you'll forgive me. God loves you, and may the Lord bless you." You should have seen that man's face change gears!

Don't ever let anybody curse you without your blessing them. God can't do anything but purpose good intent, and he wants us to bless. That's the supreme purpose of God. He has chosen us in Christ to bless us with every spiritual blessing in the heavenlies.

Some time ago I was at a filling station getting my auto wheels balanced for a long trip. The fellow doing the work was getting exasperated, and he was damning the wheels. I said to him, "Now, my dear brother, you know I've got a long trip, and really, I need some blessed wheels. Listen, I don't want cursed wheels. Let's stop and bless these wheels. I take it that you've damned everything in your shop. These tools—they need to be blessed. Let's bless everything."

So I proceeded to bless the wheels, bless his tools, bless him, and bless the station employees. When we got into the car for a road test he said, "You know, I really appreciate that. My father is a Church of God preacher, and he's been praying for me."

The wrath of God is operative for those who are outside Jesus Christ. They simply kick against the goad. Our generation is living under the wrath of God, and this present world is under his righteous judgment. What do we mean by that? For one thing, God's wrath is revealed by withholding wisdom from the leadership of nations. How can we explain such tragic mistakes as Yalta, Potsdam, Cuba, Formosa, Vietnam, Cambodia, and, more recently, Watergate? Otherwise learned, brilliant, and erudite men make such tragic blunders because they live outside the divine enlightenment and under the wrath of God. Outside Christ, life gets muddled. One cannot live progressively and creatively while going against life's true destiny, against one's predestination.

Actually, predestination has to do with the church, those who are in Christ. This term has no meaning to a world outside Christ. When we step by faith into Christ, we step into our true destiny. But if we remain outside Christ's control, we live under his wrath. That is the nature of things, as water is wet and growing grass is green.

That is the reason God commands us to pray for our rulers. Condemnation and criticism will only entangle them more deeply in their negative impulses. "I exhort you therefore that first of all supplication, prayers, intercessions and giving of thanks be made for all men, kings, and all those who are in authority that we may lead a quiet and peaceful life in all godliness and honesty (I Tim. 2:1-2). Leaders need our prayers so that peace may prevail and the gospel may have free access through the public media. Through the prayers of the church even godless rulers can be moved to serve God's purposes. God can make the wrath of men to praise him. But the wrath of God prevails over the world of rebellious men.

The wrath of God rests upon every new achievement, and every new discovery is marked with perilous and sadistic designs as the nations cast up their mire and dirt. That's the background. "But God, who is rich in mercy, out of the great love with which he loved us, even when we were dead through our trespasses, made us alive together with Christ (by grace you have been saved) and raised us up with him in the heavenly places in Christ Jesus" (see Eph. 2:4-6).

Deliverance: The Energy Conquest

This but God follows some very excited and tumultuous Greek sentences. Note, for example, the sentence beginning in Ephesians 1:18. When the apostle starts this sentence it comes like a torrent. Notice also there is no full stop, just commas. It's all one great sentence. It comes like a hallelujah chorus. Paul seems not to be able to stop it. It cascades. He strains at the leash of language as he puts an immense vocabulary under the tribute of his scintillating mind.

Please read it aloud and feel the pulse of it. The first verse of chapter 2 says, "You hath he quickened." Those words are italic, which means that they are not in the original Greek. They have been put there by the translators to give the sense of the text. Doubtless the translators thought they had best bring us back to earth after Paul's tumultuous ending of chapter 1. I think they did us a good service. Let us notice what Paul wrote in verse 20. "Which he wrought in Christ, when he raised him from the dead, and set him at his own right hand in the heavenly places, far above all principality and power, and might, and dominion, and every name that is named, not only in this world, but also in that which is to come" (Eph. 1:20).

Verse one of chapter 2: *And you* he made alive." He raised Christ *and you.* Please get hold of that. Christ was dead; God raised him from the dead. You were dead; God raised you from the dead. God seated him at his own right hand above all principalities and powers, mights, dominions, and every name that is named. And now God has seated you with him. Together! Him and you!

If we ever get the idea that he is up yonder somewhere in a dimension far removed, while we are down here trying to get our prayers through, we have lost the meaning of Christian prayer. He raised Christ and us, and now we are sitting together in heavenly places.

Heavenly in this context means a new order or a new dimension of reality over which Jesus Christ presides. The Father has set him above all principalities and powers. His divine footprint of sovereignty is upon the neck of evil as he tramps out the vintage where the grapes of wrath are stored! He *is* reigning.

I cannot tell you how this transformed my ministry when it came as dawn to my eyes and music to my ears. I recited the Apostles' Creed, "He ascended into heaven." And yet how easy to have trafficked in unfelt truth. I had said it, I had known it, but I had not realized it. Jesus is reigning now!

> He reigns! Ye saints exalt your strains.
> Your God is King, your Father reigns.
> And He is at the Father's side,
> The Man of love, the Crucified.
> (Geoffrey King, *Truth for Our Times*
> [Grand Rapids: Eerdmans Publishing Co., 1957])

Jesus was crucified nineteen hundred years ago as the sin-bearer, substitute, and savior. Now, at this present moment in time, he is the top man of this universe—supreme in heaven, supreme over earth, supreme over hell.

> Jesus! the name high over all,
> In hell or earth or sky;
> Angels and men before it fall,
> And devils fear and fly. (Charles Wesley)

Do we believe this? When Jesus Christ returns, he will not come to do something that he has not already done. He has already finished everything. He has triumphed. When he comes back, it will be to unveil what has already been accomplished. That is the hope of the church, not of the world. Calvary is the hope of the world, but the second coming of Jesus Christ is the hope of his church.

He reigns now. If we want that truth reinforced we have only to read Ephesians 1, Colossians 1, Hebrews 1, and Revelation 1. He reigns in us. He reigns in the heavenlies. The heavenlies is not some ethereal world of the might-be or ideal world of the should-be but the nuclear world of the now-is. "Thine is the kingdom," not going to be. It is!

Two things turn on this truth. First, when Christ came out of the grave, a whole new humanity came out with him. This is the meaning of the church. Paul exhausts the vocabulary of power to describe the resurrection of Jesus from the dead.

33

Four of the most dynamic words of the Greek language are used here: *power, working, strength,* and *might,* in that order. They express the greatest output of energy in the whole Bible. As if that were not enough, Paul adds "the exceeding greatness" of his power. All this to raise Jesus from the dead. It took power to do that, more power than it took to create all the galaxies, to roll back the waters of the Red Sea, to bring down the bastions of Jericho. It took the might of supreme majesty to raise Jesus from the dead, and this is the power given to us who believe. This is the power that converted Saul of Tarsus, and it is the power that can convert this world and bring it back to God. I know the situation today is desperate, dark, and dismal. A man said to one of our church members, "Why don't you get out of your denominational church? It's dead." His quick reply was, "That may be, but God hasn't appointed me as the undertaker."

The second thing is that there were those who opposed Christ. We read this in the fourth chapter of Ephesians. When God raised Jesus from the dead, he led captivity captive and gave gifts unto men. The Bible teaches that Jesus passed right through the headquarters of the powers of darkness. All the serried ranks of hell's forces opposed him, but Jesus passed right through them and took the righteous into paradise with him. He led captivity captive.

> He hath crush'd beneath His rod
> The world's proud rebel king,
> He plunged in His imperial strength
> To gulfs of darkness down.
> He brought His trophy up at length,
> The foil'd usurper's crown. (Mrs. Cousin,
>   "To Thee, and to Thy Christ")

What happened historically also happens experientially. Christ descends into the depths of our personalities. He finds there feelings, memories, impulses that are God created.

They were meant to find expression in joy, in hope, and in helpfulness. But they are bound like Lazarus. Lazarus brought his graveclothes out of the grave with him. Jesus left his graveclothes behind when he emerged from Joseph's tomb. So Christ comes to lift the human ego out of its old wrappings, out of the bondage of the past, out of the fear of the future, and out of the inadequacy of the present.

Christ sets the captive free—free from distressful and hurtful wounds, free from the dark pictures hung in the gallery of the mind. He moves down in the subliminal depths, opening windows long sealed, allowing the sunlight of heaven to pour through. He sweeps away the shame of ancient memories. All the creative impulses are set free and activated. We are free to live positively, purposefully, productively. He captures man's soul!

Then, says the writer, "He that descended is the same also that ascended up far above all heavens, that he might fill all things" (Eph. 4:10). When the Lord Jesus from the heights, descended into the depths and then ascended into the heights, he did it in order to get hold of those who are captives, to break their captivity, and then to put them in captivity of himself. Thus he lifts us to where he is so that, as we ascend with him, we begin to reign over life's murky moods and carnal proclivities and besieging problems.

In the treasury of my God-given and great-hearted friends in Christ is Dr. Helen Roseveare, medical missioner with World Evangelization Crusade. From her own lips she shared with me the account of that awful night of October 29, 1964 (in what was then Congo), when rebel soldiers dragged her out, cruelly beat her, and were intent on her death. In the midst of that awfulness and wickedness and cruelty, she suddenly realized Christ was reigning over her, and all the insurrectionary forces were under his control.

Suddenly I knew with every fiber of my being that God was there, the whole Trinity, the total God, reigning in all his majesty! I knew

35

he was in charge and the rebels could not touch me without his permission. I was overwhelmed with the high sense of privilege to be his ambassador. For twenty years I had the privilege of asking and receiving. Anything I had wanted, God had granted. But that night, the almighty Creator stooped to ask of me something that he appeared to need. He asked me for the loan of my body. And I had the overwhelming sense of the inestimable privilege of sharing with him in some little way, just the edge of the fellowship of his sufferings.

God had the initiative, even in that dark night of persecution.

This is the eternal relevance of Christ's ascension linked to our human dilemma. He comes down to where we are, bringing his throne so that, when the human tendency is to say "All hell's breaking loose," the higher alternative is "All heaven's breaking in!"

God's Big Idea

G. K. Chesterton has observed that there is one great mystery in nature, something too bright for us to look at, namely, the sun. There it hangs in the sky in blazing and blinding majesty, yet in the light of that sun, everything else is made clear.

That is what we have in the revelation of God's Word. Down through the ages men have been blinded by its brilliant light and glory. But in the light of his Word, everything else about God, about man, about destiny has been made clear.

It is this kind of illumination of the human mind and heart for which Paul prays in Ephesians 1:15-18: "Wherefore I also, after I heard of your faith in the Lord Jesus, and love unto all the saints, cease not to give thanks for you ... that the God of our Lord Jesus Christ, the Father of glory, may give unto you the spirit of wisdom and revelation ... the eyes of your understanding being enlightened."

God's Getting Down to Earth

Paul is here commending the Ephesians for their faith and love. Then suddenly he prays, "Now I want you Ephesian Christians to get your eyes opened. Although you have justifying faith and sanctifying love, there is yet a further need. You must have insight. I want you to see the mystery." It is this revelation that has to touch the church again before we can know the exceeding greatness of God's power operating through us. That illumination must touch our understanding. We are dull and we need our natural faculties heightened and enhanced.

I am convinced we can go no further without revelation.

Revelation doesn't affront our reason but affirms it. The mind was not given to make us brilliant any more than the Law was given to make the Jews just. The Law was given to take the Jews by the hand and lead them to grace. They perverted it by making it an end.

The human mind was given to lead us to revelation, to make us realize the ultimate necessity of wisdom from above. But, instead, we make the mind to be ultimate. We read in the first chapter of Romans that when man saw God in the created order, man glorified Him not as God. Instead, man became vain in his imagination; his foolish heart was darkened. Professing himself to be wise, he became a fool, because man elevated the mind to be the ultimate arbiter of all things, instead of God.

We think we can understand God with the mind, but the mind is an instrument of guidance, not the guide. It is the great sorting house, but it is not the sorter. It is given to us that we might be given illumination by the Spirit of wisdom and revelation. We need both: revelation is objective—it relates to truth; wisdom is subjective—it relates to life. Wisdom is an understanding of how to make the revelation apply in life's situations. Revelation is given so that the church may not only realize its inheritance through Christ in heaven but that Christ might have his inheritance through the church on earth.

Samuel Chadwick, that inestimable Methodist of England and former principal of Cliff College, once prayed, "Lord, make me intensely spiritual, thoroughly practical, and perfectly natural." God's revelation enables us to walk worthily and to fulfill the ethical content of our gospel.

We must see that the end to which God has called us is not to get to heaven when we die. He calls us to be the church right now, to be the medium whereby the kingdom of God might come on earth as it is in heaven, in the now.

Rufus Moseley was fond of saying: "What God was, he is.

What God said, he says. What God did, he does." A dear
southern preacher said, "God's no *was*-er. He's an *is*-er."

Much of the inheritance God has for us in the now, we
have pushed on ahead to the shadowland of death and into
the gloryland of heaven. The goal of God is not to get man to
heaven but to get the God of heaven into man, to produce
Christian character, and to restore the true content of our
humanity, which is Christ in us, the hope of glory. This is a
mystery. That word *mystery* is not the false spirituality of the
gnostic (*gnostic*—a heresy of the first Christian centuries
which taught that knowledge was the way of salvation and
that the spiritual was separate from and superior to the realm
of physical reality), not some esoteric quality in which only
the spiritually elite can participate. No, it is a mystery for all
mankind that the same God who became man in Jesus has
come to live that perfect life all over again through his
church.

I like to think of the Holy Spirit as the third person of the
Trinity—God without a body, seeking a body, clothing
himself as divine activity—in the failing flesh of the church,
raising it up, and implementing the eternal purpose for
which we were born again.

The divine Person of the Godhead has already lived out
this perfect life, has met every temptation, exigency,
contingency, extremity, and adversity. You and I will never
have to meet an experience that he has not already
mastered. He now offers that same life to be lived all over
again in and through us.

Someone said, "I don't believe that Jesus Christ can
possibly understand my tribulation. After all, Jesus lived in a
different day. Jesus never knew what it was to be married. He
never had a flat tire. He never got caught in an airplane in a
snowstorm."

My response is that all these aforementioned things are
but varying forms of human frustration, and Jesus, indeed,
met human frustration. He met it in the adequacy of the Holy

Spirit, and he says, "I want to give to you the same Holy Spirit."

It is no hidden secret that Christ would come, would bear the sins of many, and would become a Prince and a Savior. Nor is it a secret that the Holy Spirit would be outpoured, nor, that the remission of sins would be preached. The mystery was that God would take Jew and Gentile, bond and free, male and female and make them one new Body, the church of Jesus Christ. The Old Testament writers didn't see this church. They hinted at it but were not explicit.

Wesley captures this thought in perhaps the greatest hymn ever written.

> And can it be that I should gain
> An interest in the Savior's blood?
> Died he for me, who caused his pain?
> For me, who him to death pursued?
> Amazing love! how can it be
> That thou, my Lord, shouldst die for me?
> ("And Can It Be That I Should Gain")

Then comes the stanza in which Wesley declares that even the angels cannot fathom the mystery:

> 'Tis mercy all! let earth adore;
> Let angel minds inquire no more.

God's will for the unity of the church, for the bringing together of the Body through which he can manifest and express himself, is the most central thing in cosmic and human history. The world moves in the context of church history. Church history does not move in the context of world affairs. God's big idea is the church, and, therefore, he is going to bring all its divisions to an end. The Bible says in Ephesians 1:10 that God will bring all things together in Jesus Christ. And in the tenth verse of the third chapter, Paul says God is going to show to all principalities and powers his immutable wisdom in choosing his church. This is something wonderful!

Faith Releases God's Activity

The mission of the church is predicated in victory. What exploits we would plan if we really knew we could not fail! Yet this is the case. On every battlefield, his church is winning out. I like the aggressiveness of the New Testament; not one paragraph is reserved for defeat. Bethlehem's morn is God's answer to this world's scorn. God has fleshed it out in Jesus Christ. I thank God that he is fleshing it out again in the church which is his Body, the fullness of him that filleth all in all. "Christ in you the hope of glory." The mystery is that he would go back to heaven, become a King incognito, preside over his church, gather up his Body, and through that Body put all things under his feet. Thus, he is redeeming the world, not apart from us but through us.

Finally, he will appear with his church to smite the Antichrist with the brightness of his coming. As Sidlow Baxter often says, following such a triumphant note, "Excuse me, but hallelujah!"

When we say "Christ in you," what do we mean? What part of the anatomy comes to mind? When we say "Christ dwells in my heart," a lot of folk point to their physical cardiac. They mean the blood pump. We talk about the center of our emotions being the heart. But a missionary friend informs me that in Africa there is a tribe that considers the liver to be the center of life. Instead of saying "I love you with all my heart," they would say, "I love you with all my liver."

What is Paul talking about when he says "that Christ may dwell in your heart"? He's speaking of Christ's dwelling in human nature. You and I, alone in God's creation, have the capacity to receive God in our human nature. That is why the incarnation was possible—man is made in the image of God, and God has an affinity with humanity.

And didst Thou love the race that loved not Thee?
And didst Thou take to heaven a human brow?
Dost plead with man's voice by the marvellous sea?
Art Thou his Kinsman now?   (King, *Truth for Our Times*)

Yes, thank God, he is our kinsman! Our Kinsman-Redeemer. The universal God who fills all things came down in the scandal of the particular, the incarnation. In so doing he did not lay aside his deity. He took our humanity, the particular, back up to the universal, and now there is a man on the throne of the universe. He did not lay aside our humanity when he went back into heaven. Heaven and earth are married in the incarnation and resurrection and ascension glory.

We have the capacity to receive God in our human nature. When the Word of God is preached, it is quick and powerful and sharp; it divides soul and spirit and restores the true spiritual nature of man. (See Heb. 4:12.) It revives man's spirit; God infuses his life. This is what the new birth is about. When the Word of God is preached, faith is born, for "faith cometh by hearing and hearing by the Word." Faith releases the life of God in the human spirit; and man lives again.

John Henry Jowett tells about an old reprobate who was converted. His eye had been shot out in a drunken brawl, but this man now had the life of Christ in him. Jowett described the man as looking like "a half-ruined old cathedral lit up for evening service."

As Christ invades the human spirit, he turns us on to life.

As a boy of seventeen I had this quickening. I was just droning along in complacency, vagabonding among half loyalties, loitering through life. I had no overriding purpose. And then, the Word of God came! As John Masefield wrote:

I knew that Christ had given me birth,
To brother all the souls on earth.
(*Everlasting Mercy* [The Macmillan Co., n.d.])

Christ in you. This is the mystery. When the human spirit and the divine spirit are reunited, we know we have been baptized into one Body, we are made to drink of one Spirit. We come alive to God and become conscious that we are in a fellowship that is supranational and extra-terrestrial.

I thank God for my own particular communion. In it I have a rich heritage. But I am thankful for this gospel that's transcendent. The late Dr. E. Stanley Jones was once asked, "Do you belong to the Methodists?" He replied, "No, they belong to me. For all things are mine in Christ."

I'm thankful to be free to explore the great expanse of Christian fellowship. I don't want to be a little shrimp confined to one small puddle. I want to explore the great ocean. God has put us in the Body. I see in the world today that Body of Christ coming to life, transcending all denominations. Thank God that he has used historic denominations as a launching pad for some of us. But I'm a true ecumenist. I believe in showing the multifaceted comprehensive love of God, which not any one of us can do separately. "I bow my knee unto the Father of our Lord Jesus Christ, from whom the whole family in heaven and earth is named." The whole family! Heaven and earth!

What a wonderful fellowship is found when we come into Jesus Christ. It is a worldwide, globe-circling entity. We may go to any city, to any country. We don't meet strangers; we meet members of the family.

This is a glorious truth. It keeps us humble, because truth is angular. I don't have *all* the truth, only an angle on it. I look at it from this perspective. Another comes at it from a different angle. And here's another person looking at it from yet another vantage. Together we comprehend the breadth and length and depth and height so that we come to know the love of Christ which surpasses knowledge. (See Eph. 3:16.) That's the mystery.

Fitting Us for Heaven and Earth

We are initiated into this mystery through the new birth in which there is an *infusion* of life. God intends this to result in a *suffusion* whereby all this earthly part of us is filled with the life of God. That's what sanctification is all about. Justification sets us free from guilt and gives us a right standing before God, makes us fit for heaven. But sanctification releases the life of God in us, making us fit for earth. We are not fit for earth until we're filled with all the fullness of the Holy Spirit who exalts Christ as Lord in our lives.

If my arm could be detached from my body and then grafted back, that would be the baptism of the arm into the body. But after that arm is grafted back, the life of the whole body has to flow in its fullness into my arm, so it partakes of the same life as does the whole body.

That's what we commonly refer to as the baptism in the Holy Spirit, but I like to refer to it as the fullness of the Holy Spirit, because the promise of Jesus to baptize us is realized in the release of his fullness. Fullness! "That ye might be filled." This is the fullness that God is giving the church today, taking our personalities and integrating them around a new center, taking the life of Christ and making him available to us and making us adequate in that life, gathering up all conflicting loyalties, and putting life under the control of the Holy Spirit. That's a very practical thing.

A friend told me about a man who was seeking the deeper experience of holiness in his life. He and his wife were questing for God's best, and finally they came to the place where there was released in them and in their innermost being the fullness of the Holy Spirit. It just began to flow. He said, "I know my wife received the Holy Spirit last week." "How do you know?" my friend asked. "Because she now puts the top back on the toothpaste, that's how I know."

My friends, that is both sensible and scriptural. This woman was scattered and fragmented, but now she's integrated. She's beginning to get it all together. And that's what the Holy Spirit had accomplished in the deep recesses of her being. Being full of God, the conflicting loyalties are gone.

Fullness means that we have the same mind as Christ, we have his gracious influence. The Holy Spirit releases in us the fullness of Christ. It's something like marriage. There's a time when one meets one's spouse-to-be and falls in love. Then there is a period of courtship and acquaintance with each other's ways. But that's not fullness. Fullness is the expanding joys of marriage.

I remember, very well, standing at the altar of the church in 1949, looking at my wife-to-be as she came down the aisle. I stood there waiting (supported by twelve preachers). Soon I was saying yes to her and no to everyone else.

At that moment, I could say I was full of her life as I had never been before. It was a crucial moment of filling. How foolish I would have been to have stood there weeping, because I was attaching myself to one woman when I could have been such a blessing to so many! I was now united in a oneness that ended all pluralism and caused me to say, "This one thing I do!"

The Holy Spirit comes to unite us with Jesus Christ so that his gracious life may fill our lives. He does not destroy our true humanity, our true selfhood; he heightens it, cleanses it, purges it of selfishness, self-mindedness, double-mindedness. He breathes his gracious influence into our lives and puts life under the benign theocracy of a new order—the kingdom of God.

The measure of fullness has to get into every part of us. It is absolutely necessary, because we don't have control over our subliminal depths—over our actions, yes, but not over our reactions.

Fullness means Christ's settled residence, touching the depths of our emotional lives. A part of man's soul is emotion. We should not minimize emotion.

But God does not perform his deepest work in the most shallow part of man. His deepest work is in the depths of man's personality, in the mind realm. That is the reason Paul admonishes us to look to the Holy Spirit for the renewing of our minds. (See Eph. 4:23.)

The Mystery
That Masters Our Manners

We come now to a consideration of the mastery by which we are controlled. In Ephesians 3:16 is the prayer: "That according to the riches of his glory he may grant you to be strengthened with might through his Spirit in the inner man." The divine Spirit merges with the human spirit, as the water is in the sponge and the sponge is in the water, as the fire is in the poker and the poker is in the fire. So is Christ in us, not destroying our personality, but cleansing it, coordinating it, putting it under a new control, and giving us the authentic expression of our true identity.

We can't even know ourselves until we get in Christ, because our true identity is revealed in him. We were chosen in Christ before the foundation of the world. Subsequently we died with him and were raised with him and were seated with him and are yet to appear with him. That is why we can't know ourselves apart from him.

The Mystery

Christ in you, the hope of glory. That is the basic proposition of the Christian faith. William Law once said, "This is the whole gospel: the birth of the lowly Lord Jesus Christ in you, his overcoming life conquering your inward death." True, it is a mystery how one personality can merge and intermingle with another. But it is an open secret in which everyone may participate.

I relinquish myself; he releases what he is, in me. He does not destroy; he strengthens with might by his Spirit in the inner man (now watch the transition), "in order that Christ may *dwell*." This means that Christ now takes up his settled residence, not just a visitor for the night, not just meeting us at church or convocation time, not just getting on the mountaintop with an emotional lift.

I do not want to minimize emotion. People's emotions have been starved too long, and I am glad for a new surge of spontaneity these days. I don't want to go on feeling, but I sure want to feel what I'm going on. We are not cold fish—we are warm-blooded mammals.

> Feelings come and feelings go,
> And feelings are deceiving.
> Our warrant is the Word of God,
> None else is worth believing. (Origin unknown)

I'm absolutely convinced that the Holy Spirit superintended the writing of his Word. Many assume this. But for many of us there have been times when that assumption had to be tested. I have been through theological studies that have wrested my mind, and I have felt like Blaise Pascal when he said, "The heart has reasons that the reason knows nothing about." There was something that transcended my reason. I laid aside these problems but later had them resolved as I took a devotional disposition toward the Word of God.

There is no doubt in my thinking that the Holy Spirit guided the translation and the transmission of the biblical text so that we have the right words. One can call it verbal inspiration or whatever. I am convinced that we have the words in this Book that God desired. If we did not, we would have no authoritative message.

A certain company sent a note to its constituency which was supposed to have read: "We *take* a personal interest in all our customers." But because of a typographical error the message was: "We *fake* a personal interest in all our customers."

I do not believe God allowed that kind of error to happen

in these original manuscripts. I know there are variations in translations. I've had a bit of education along these lines, but I am convinced that God has given us an inerrant translation of his Word so that, pertaining to essential doctrine, we have in the Bible the truth of God upon which we can depend.

The Mastery

So meticulous was the Holy Spirit who chose the word *Christos*. That is the way the passage reads in Ephesians 3:14-18: "That *Christ* may dwell in your hearts." Christ—not the Lord, not Jesus, but Christ. *Christos* means the "Anointed One," the One who was born to be king, the One who has a right to be king. The business of the Holy Spirit, in strengthening us with might in the inner man, is that Christ, the anointed one, might be enthroned in totalitarian sovereignty in our lives. Fullness and mastery go hand in hand. Here again is the message of the fourth chapter of Ephesians: Christ ascended and led captivity captive; he went down into the depths and brought up a multitude of captives. What he did historically, empirically, he does experientially. He goes down into the depths of the human personality and releases whatever is captive. Our minds have been captivated by false ideas, false impressions. A multitude of captives clamor in the subliminal depths of our personality. When the Holy Spirit comes, he releases us from this captivity and we become our true selves. We are bound to him, and he gives us his gifts so that the Body may be completed and come to full stature. Such a church expresses the totality of his being. He sets us free in order that he might put us back under the proper Authority. *Christos* gives us the mastery of life.

In the seventh chapter of Luke a centurion came to Jesus, wanting his servant healed (vv. 1-10). He said to Jesus, "I am not worthy that thou shouldst enter under my roof. . . . But say in a word . . ."

That centurion said to Jesus, "Your word is as good as your presence. You say in a word, and my servant will be healed."

This centurion knew what authority meant. There was a time when he knelt before Caesar and kissed the scepter. He rose to his feet and his life was no longer his own. He was a man under authority; he would go where Caesar appointed him. He had no more options as far as the clothes he would wear or the people he would meet or the circumstances under which he would live; he was a slave to Caesar.

Being under such authority, the centurion had authority. He could say to soldiers "Come," and they would come; "Go," and they would go; "Do this," and they would do it. "But," the centurion said, "my authority is limited. I also am a man under authority. I am an *also* man; but you, Jesus, are an *absolute* man. Your authority is unlimited."

Being bound to Christ, we limit ourselves to his unlimitedness. That is the proposition of the gospel. It is not "Christ first" but "Christ only."

Herein lies the serious problem in our organizational church today. We are trying to exercise authority without being under Christ's authority. When Jesus is Lord, when we capitulate to his indwelling lordship, then we become men and women of true authority. We can say to men "Come," and they will come.

In the New Testament, evangelism was not something people had to be implored to do. Today we sit in our conferences and say, "Now we've got to win people to Christ," and we set our goals and make our plans.

In the New Testament we see a church getting in touch with its exalted Head, the Lord Jesus Christ. They're not asking people "Are you saved?" People are asking them "What must we do to be saved?"

That was true in Jesus' ministry. When the rich young ruler came to him, Jesus didn't say, "Now, look, you don't have what I have. You lack something. Let me tell you what it is."

That rich young ruler had everything. He was moral. He was mannerly. He had endowments that are greatly to be desired. But he saw in Jesus authority that he didn't have. And so the rich young ruler asked, "What lack I yet?"

Consider Paul and Silas in jail. They were not passing out tracts or attempting to convert the jailer. They were in touch with their exalted Head, the Lord Jesus Christ. They entered into a state of praise and adoration—praise for what God had done and adoration for what he is. They were "lost in wonder, love, and praise," as Wesley phrased it. At that moment the Lord manifested himself and the jailer asked, "Sirs, what must I do to be saved?"

Philip, joining that chariot in the desert, intercepted the Ethiopian eunuch. The man bowed to the claims of Christ's lordship, and what happened? Philip didn't say, "Now, my brother, you have made a confession, and you've got to be baptized." The Ethiopian saw some water and asked, "What doth hinder me?"

Evangelism is not something that is mandatory or voluntary; it is inevitable.

> What we have felt and seen
> With confidence we tell;
> And publish to the sons of men
> The signs infallible. (Charles Wesley, "How Can a Sinner Know")

Few of us realize how much our church and Western democracy owe to the Wesleyan movement. That heritage is predicated upon the experience of one man. This clergyman conducted himself properly before the altar of the Church of England, but his heart was crying out for the fullness of the blessing of the gospel. He came to America to convert the Indians, but John Wesley had no authority that would subdue them. So he went back to England a disillusioned man.

John Wesley felt that the shrine of the great invitation had been the established Church of England. He thought it a vile thing to go outside the church to witness or to preach. A vile thing!

But George Whitefield was preaching throughout the land, laying people under the claim of Christ, and reducing scores to submission before the invisible throne. Whitefield, having only one good lung, was preaching to ten thousand people in the open air. The late William E. Sangster observed, Whitefield was so cross-eyed that when he said "that man," two men would come under conviction!

Then came that eventful evening of May 24, 1738, at quarter of nine. We debate what happened to Wesley at Aldersgate—his conversion or sanctification. It matters not. What counts is that there came to his heart a new certainty about Jesus Christ. John Wesley emerged from that rendezvous with God, put one foot over his horse, and rode off to the conquest of England. Later he wrote in his journal, "I consented to become more vile and to preach the Gospel in the open air."

What happened to John Wesley? The Evangel, the Lord Jesus Christ, had been elevated to ascendency in his heart. That Evangel was going to preach whether or not John Wesley the cleric wanted to!

The late Dr. Dale, the Congregationalist, of Birmingham, England, offered the insight that Wesley considered himself a *servant* before Aldersgate but then came into a consciousness of *sonship* on that occasion. Whatever it was, it gave a sharp edge to his ministry, and Wesley cut out from the ecclesiastical wilderness of his day the timbers that were to comprise the bulwark of a church in which God was to enthrone himself and set England ablaze with ten thousand tongues singing "my great Redeemer's praise, the glories of

my God and King, the triumphs of his grace" (Charles
Wesley, "O For A Thousand Tongues to Sing").

If, in our churches, we will get people under God's
authority, we can turn them loose for service. We don't have
to bother about preaching on the mini-issues and transfixing
them on trifles.

When I went to my present appointment twenty-one years
ago, it soon became obvious that God's prospering hand was
upon us. It was a new community, and there were people
coming from every direction wanting to join our church.
(Someone has said that Americans are notorious joiners—
give them a red button and a certificate and they'll join
anything!) Some of them wanted to move their church letters
from the Baptist graveyard to the Methodist mausoleum. We
felt that these dear people needed the concept of the church
that is given in the Ephesian epistle, so we began teaching
membership classes on what the church *is* when the church
is the Church. In this, the biblical concept of the church was
clearly delineated.

I'll never forget one fellow who called and wanted to join
the church. I put him off for a spell, asking him to come and
expose himself to this teaching. He was under very deep
conviction and in my study surrendered his life to Christ.
When he arose from his knees he looked out the window
and said, "My, everything looks brand-new!" I replied, "It is
brand-new; you're in the kingdom of God." Then he reached
for his pocketbook, directly in his hip pocket. He took out
some money and thrust it at me. Never having had this
happen before, I didn't know whether to take it.

I learned something that day: there's a nerve that goes
from the heart, right down to the wallet. And ever since that
time, I have had a new insight on stewardship. It is a reflex
that occurs when that nerve is struck! Jesus is Lord that
Christ may dwell in your hearts by faith. The *mystery* of it,
yes, but the *mastery* of it is "that Christ may dwell in your

hearts." The manner of it is "that Christ may dwell in your hearts by faith."

The Manner

What is faith? Faith is pure receptivity. The law of faith is: "What we take takes us." If you take food into your body, what happens? It takes you. If it's poison, too bad, you've got it. No, you haven't; it's got you.

I take a seat; the seat takes me. I take an idea into my mind; an idea takes me. That's the reason it's absolutely imperative that we preach sound doctrine. Paul says that evil communications corrupt good manners. If our teaching is wrong, then our acting will be wrong.

It is tragic that we have allowed this generation to think the Ten Commandments to be something superimposed on the social order. These commandments were never meant to be given solely in a negative vein. Read the preamble to the Ten Commandments! "I am the Lord who delivered thee," therefore, this is the way delivered people will act. He is saying, "Be what you are, God's redeemed people." When we respond to that, then God releases the divine energy.

Jesus said to the man with the withered hand, "Stretch forth thine hand" (Mark 3:5). The man couldn't do it, but when he began to obey, the Word of Christ was like a bridge over which the power of Christ traveled, enabling that man to do what he was commanded to do. Augustine said it this way: "Lord, give what Thou commandest and then command what Thou wilt."

When God says to us "Be not drunk with wine, . . . but be filled with the Spirit" (Eph. 5:18), when God says "Be strong in the Lord, and in the power of his might" (Eph. 6:10), he is saying "Be what you really are in Christ."

To whom is he addressing these words? Weak people. And on what authority are we to be strong? The authority of the Word of the living God. That is, when he asks us to do something, he has already provided the strength in us to do it. That's the reason he says, "Before they call, I will answer" (Isa. 65:24). For every need we have, the supply is already there—even before the need arises. And by faith we receive. By faith we enter into it. By faith we are what God ordained us to be in the present, continuous sense. For he says, "Keep on being filled." "The just shall live by faith" (Rom. 1:17), not *believe* by faith but *live* by faith. Reginald Wallace once said the greatest discovery he ever made was that he could not live the Christian life and that God never expected him to! What God really expected of him was a response to the living Christ that Wallace might be filled with the Holy Spirit.

Samuel Chadwick said, "I never knew my need of the Holy Spirit until I was flung up against impossible circumstances, and God exposed my utter, absolute bankruptcy. When he did, I cried out to God and was filled."

Our fullness is based on our receptivity, and our receptivity on our sense of need. All the fitness God requires is to feel our need of him.

"Blessed are they which do hunger and thirst after righteousness, for they shall be filled." The promise is to the hungry, to the thirsty.

I saw a cartoon depicting two camels in the desert. One turned to the other and said, "I don't care what anybody says, I'm thirsty."

The whole purpose of the preaching of the gospel is to incite that thirst. As we preach, people begin to say, "Why, I didn't even know God had *that* to offer." They begin to get excited. Hunger begins to rise within them, and they cry out to God for fullness.

One of the great saints of the church, Andrew Bonar, said, "To never thirst is to ever thirst." As we ever thirst, we ever receive. We take. And as we take, he takes us. It's a continual process of traveling between our weakness and his strength and appropriating him in a daily walk.

It is wonderful to wake up every morning and greet each

new dawn, saying, "Lord Jesus, I don't know what will happen to me today, but I know that whatever happens has to be for the best, because my life is ordered of you. And every demand upon me today is a demand on you in me. And I thank you, Lord Jesus, that you have raised me from the dead today. I'm a resurrected personality."

It takes a lot of faith to fall asleep and leave everything in the hands of another. When you were asleep, for all practical purposes, you were dead, but God has raised you to a new dawn. He says, "I want to send you out today with the total adequacy and mastery and victory of my life in you."

The only time we have any business worrying and fretting and becoming anxious is when we meet a problem that's bigger than the one God solved when he raised his Son from the dead. If we get into that kind of situation, we should worry! But otherwise, "be ye filled with the Spirit," the other self of our risen Lord.

The Unifying Purpose

We live in a standardized, collectivized, computerized generation that insists upon uniformity. But our uniformity does not succeed in unifying our race. I heard about a fellow who went to the doctor for treatment of a sore toe. He only wanted the doctor to look at the toe, diagnose the trouble, and prescribe a remedy. But before this could be done the nurse had him filling out all manner of medical forms. "But," he protested, "all I want is the doctor to take a quick look at my toe." The nurse insisted that this was standard procedure and shuffled him off into a side room where he was to don a gown and wait for the doctor. He was protesting vigorously when a comrade (with a thermometer in his mouth) in the adjoining room overheard and called, "Why don't you stop complaining. At least you have a sore toe. I just came in here to fix the telephone!"

Too much of our society today suffers from an attempt to regiment people into standard procedures which result in uniformity but no unity. We sadly lack the essential unity needed for the true expression of man's communal life.

This is what Alice Armstrong Ward was protesting in her book *I Remain Unvanquished* (Nashville: Abingdon Press, 1970). In this remarkable account of a ten-year battle with cancer, in which a transcendent grace was given to triumph over pain and death, Mrs. Ward writes:

I was referred to cancer specialists at Johns Hopkins. Every three months when I went for an examination I clearly explained to them, as I had to my previous doctors, that I put neither my life nor my fate in their hands; that I had a higher loyalty in my life—the Christ within me. My body was the temple of His Spirit. I wanted them to relate to me in the same spirit. (p. 84)

What an amazing concept! This is a cry for unity, not uniformity, in which we cease treating cases and begin relating to persons.

Until we see God's purpose of a total body's functioning in the unity of the Spirit, all we will have in our church life and society will be organized indefiniteness and united confusion.

The Declared Intent

One of the most breathtaking and mind-sweeping declarations we have in all literature is Ephesians 1:10, which sets forth God's purpose, the thrilling thought that the universe, all in heaven and all on earth, might be brought into the unity of Christ.

Now that's difficult to believe. Oh, I know that it sounds good enough when repeated in church on Sunday morning. We're all in a frame of mind open to such a prospect. But try to get any other group to believe that the whole purpose of the universe, with its entire and only design, both heavenly (its spiritual aspects) and earthly (its empirical data), can be brought to unity in Christ. They simply won't believe it. And the fact is that they have found other reasons for the universe. Of course, some say there is no purpose at all and that it is futile to seek any. They simply take what they find and enjoy it, use it, and never attempt to explain it. They are the nihilists and pragmatists among us. Others find a design, but it never occurs to them to assign that unity for its definition to Jesus Christ.

But the writer of Ephesians says this is a mystery that is revealed. It calls for an inner illumination. It calls for the "eyes of your understanding to be enlightened" and for "the spirit of wisdom and revelation" to be given.

One discovers some things by scientific exploration. And that is good and proper. God has designed it so. Special revelation is not necessary for a great many discoveries. All truth is God's truth, but not all truth is saving truth. There are many people, for example, who want scientific proof of God. Scientific methods as a means of verification are very limited to measurable aspects of reality. Yet they are incapable of measuring the total aspects of life. No one has ever seen three feet of love or two pounds of justice, but we don't deny their reality. Chlorine gas cannot be measured with a microphone. One must have the proper instruments of measurement.

Paul, the writer of the Ephesian epistle, says that the purpose of the universe has come by revelation. As a matter of fact, in the first chapter which is a prayer, Paul prays for "the eyes of your understanding being enlightened; that ye may know what is the hope of his calling, and what the riches of the glory of his inheritance in the saints, and what is the exceeding greatness of his power to us-ward who believe" (vv. 18-19). The revelation given in this epistle is that God, through his church, is moving to integrate this rifted universe. And the church will become the integrating center by which it is accomplished. This is a profound, breathtaking concept, especially when we realize that we are living in a universe which has a tremendous rift right down the center of it. There is a moral cleavage, if you please, that cuts its keen and uncoverable way right through history.

The Dark Interference

Bishop Leslie Newbigin, in his book *Sin and Salvation* (London: SCM Press), says: "Wherever and whenever we look at man we find that he is full of self-contradictions. He is fighting against himself, and he is divided against his environment. He is not at peace with himself; he is not at peace with his world."

We live in a world of division, enmity, conflict, tension. There is no apparent way to ignore it or to get away from it. There is neither a culture nor a society in the world where there is no tension among groups. I heard of an island in the

South Pacific that is so small it has less than one mile of road. There were only two autos on the island. And do you know what happened? You guessed it. They had a collision.

The bigger our social, political, or ecclesiastical structure, the more our problems are multiplied and compounded. "The bigger the dog, the more the fleas."

This divisiveness in life is something that is cosmic. We have little more than an intimation of its origin in pre-mundane history. Satan, then known as Lucifer, made a breach with the harmony of heaven. He refused the limitations of his creaturehood. He drew after him not more than a third of the angels in heaven. (See Isa. 14:12; Rev. 12:4.) He established an empire independent of God and contradictory to God's intentions.

The Bible is the record of subsequent interference with God's purpose. After this disruption in heaven, the very atmosphere becomes full of principalities and powers, uncongenial to the purposes of God. It breaks upon the human family. Cain murders his own brother. Family life is fragmented. Then comes Babel and a race beleagured by confusion. God acts to consolidate a witness in the nation of Israel. But this land is soon divided, followed by exile which separates them from their promised destiny. Then God introduces something resplendently new at Pentecost. "They continued stedfastly in the apostles' doctrine and fellowship, and in breaking of bread, and in prayers. . . . And all that believed were together, and had all things common" (Acts 2:42-44). There was that beautiful expression of the Godhead. It is hardly spoken until a touch of schism breaks out, to divide and to spoil. And the rest of the New Testament is battling with this thing—division and strife—and appeals for brotherhood and fellowship. "I beseech Euodias, and beseech Syntyche, that they be of the same mind in the Lord" (Phil. 4:2). "Let this mind be in you, which was also in Christ Jesus" (Phil. 2:5), "forbearing one another in love" (Eph. 4:2). "And be ye kind one to another, tenderhearted, forgiving one another" (Eph. 4:32)—a plea for single-mindedness.

Dr. William E. Sangster is reported to have addressed his Sunday morning congregation with this invective: "Do you realize that there are many who are not in church this morning because you are?"

The obstacle to Christian faith for many is the obvious unreality of our profession. A parody of a famous hymn transfixes the indictment.

> Like a mighty tortoise
> Moves the Church of God;
> Brothers, we are treading
> Where we've always trod;
> We are all divided,
> Many bodies we,
> Very strong on doctrine,
> Weak on charity. (Quoted by David Watson in
> One in the Spirit [London: Hodder &
> Stoughton, 1973])

The primeval family, the nation of Israel, the church, and, now, the international community are all affected. Mankind has grown and the whole historic system of disruption has broken upon us.

Years ago John Newman wrote a book entitled *The Idea of the University* in which he expressed concern that the uni had disappeared from the university. There was no longer any summum bonum, he said, no supreme value governing a hierarchy of values, no center of loyalty, and, indeed, no common language. Biologists had nothing to say to physicists, and neither of them could talk to the sociologists. And so, in much university life today there is a great deal of independent study with nothing to bring it together. Isolated bits of information do not make understanding any more than all the words of a dictionary make a novel, or all the bottles on a druggist's shelf make for health. A university implies a central commitment to truth, the truth about God, about man, about the world. When this integrating truth is missing there is a *multi*versity, but not a *uni*versity.

Where there is no center for *communion*, there is a loss of *community*. We are a divided people in conflict. Each individual has turned in his own way, as the scriptures state. (See Isa. 53:6.) The fourth chapter of Ephesians was written to give us that center and to fulfill the heart-cry of a man like John Wesley who confessed his longing to have a "whole Bible for his guide, a whole Christ for his Savior, and a whole church for his communion."

The Derived Image

The longing for unity is the impulse of creation, the motivation of providence, the dynamic of sovereignty, and the design of redemption. When the Bible states that "the Lord your God is one God," that becomes the basis of everything which follows. This means more than saying God is one, as contrasted with God who is two, three, or more. It means that God is what he is in his own essentiality. There is no dichotomy in him. God's attributes are not in conflict. They are not something God has but something God is.

For example, God does not give us peace. He is our peace. Even eternal life is not something God has, it is something he is. God enters and becomes in us what we have, because of what he is. We cannot divide God. Too often we think of peace or mercy or grace or justice, independently and autonomously. Whereas, all the attributes of God are simply his acting toward us in a certain way at a certain time under a certain set of circumstances. But what God does, *all* of God does.

When man sins, for example, justice demands retribution. But that is not in conflict with the goodness of God that yearns to forgive and restore blessings. This is a bracing and beneficent truth. We know that God is love, and even his justice does not conflict with that love. So when justice has to sentence a man, love agrees with it. When love sent Jesus to die, justice agreed with it. Goodness yearns to bestow blessing; grace makes it possible by atonement. Justice unites and joins along with all the other attributes of God. So John was able to write: "If we confess our sins, he is faithful and just to forgive us our sins, and to cleanse us from all unrighteousness" (I John 1:9). He is *faithful* and *just*. We might have thought that John would have written that God is "faithful and gracious" or "faithful and good." Yet even the justice of God is consonant with his love, and both team up to ensure us of our salvation.

"The law was given by Moses, but grace and truth came by Jesus Christ" (John 1:17). We have improperly interpreted that passage. We have assumed that in the Old Testament, men were under the law. In the New Testament they are under grace. Moses brought law; Jesus Christ brought grace. But there is no such division in the Bible. That statement does not mean that Moses knew only law and that Jesus knew only grace. Before the flood, "Noah found grace in the eyes of the Lord" (Gen. 6:8). The Holy Trinity—God the Father, God the Son, and God the Holy Spirit—operate all through the Bible. As a matter of fact, we cannot understand the Old Testament unless we interpret it in terms of Jesus Christ. This is the reason I think it is absurd to assume that because one has had rabbinic training one is therefore qualified to enlighten us on Old Testament teaching. Far from it! If there is anybody who does not understand the Old Testament, it is a rabbi who has no Christian presuppositions. For we must see Jesus as the key to the whole Word of God.

Grace has been in the world from the beginning, since God created the earth. But grace found an ample channel in Jesus Christ. It is the only time grace could get through to us. He provided the perfect channel. He interpreted the grace of God perfectly, and he put the content of his own life into that grace. That is the reason the Holy Spirit could not be given until Jesus was glorified, because the whole gamut of the human life of Jesus had to go into the content of the Holy Spirit. And if the life of Jesus does not go into the content of the Holy Spirit, the result will be a queering of Pentecost. For it is the Holy Spirit's purpose to magnify the Lord Jesus Christ, always and ever to form his character in us. God is one in his essentiality.

Out of this unity of God himself arises the design for his universe. "That in the dispensation of the fulness of times he might gather together in one all things in Christ, both which are in heaven, and which are on earth; even in him" (Eph. 1:10).

So let us see in Ephesians 4 God's unifying purpose. The sixteenth verse brings it into focus. "He is the head, and on him the whole body depends. Bonded and knit together by every constituent joint, the whole frame grows through the due activity of each part, and builds itself up in love" (NEB).

The Destined Integration

It is God's plan to have on earth one Body which will become the integrating center of this unity for all mankind. This Body will be the temple of his Spirit and the bride of his Son. It is to this temple that all the nations of the earth will come and light their torches of truth, not the temple of the Old Testament but the temple which is the church of Jesus Christ.

The church is the grandest concept that God ever had, for it is to be an expression of the Lord Jesus Christ himself. It will function as a living, loving, growing, learning organism that goes on to perfection, which is the maturity of character, expressing the very nature and mind of Christ.

This is not what the church *ought* to be. The Christian faith is not an *ideal* to which we aspire, it is rather a *reality* to which we adjust. The church is to adapt to the reality of its calling. It is called to belong to Christ as the body belongs to the head. It resembles a well-coordinated body. This means, of course, a unity in diversity. We can by our organizational structures and human manipulations produce *uniformity*, but it is only the Spirit of God who can create *unity*.

We have attempted to achieve this unity by forcing mankind together by fortuity, fashioning them together by federalism, tying them together by treaties, subduing them together by superstitution, huddling them together by hysteria. But it is only the church of Jesus Christ that can blend people together by brotherhood. That is Paul's thesis in the fourth chapter, because the church is that whole community of those who, by participation in the risen life of Jesus Christ, are united to one Head, who have been baptized into one Body, who are loyal to one Master, who are fired by one passion and bent on one mission. This community is made visible by the varied forms of worship and the different patterns of ministry that we shall subsequently consider. The New Testament knows nothing of that invisible church that has no local base and expression. It is not an invisible church that preaches the gospel, administers the sacraments, visits the sick, feeds the hungry, and "breaks bread together with gladness and singleness of heart."

In an address to a pastors' conference, a missionary statesman reported 163 Protestant denominations and sects in his country. That afternoon, in a discussion group, one of the men stood up and, responding to the aforementioned 163 denominations, said, "I want you to know that I don't belong to any of them." Quick as a flash the speaker replied, "Then you are the 164th!"

In order to constitute the church, there has to be an identification with a local body under New Testament–conceived and Holy Spirit–controlled leadership. We have heard it said that men are born alone, they die alone, and they come to Christ alone. If one is attempting to emphasize that each man must experience Christ for himself, this is a valid conviction. But, otherwise, it is the very acme of absurdity. What kind of biological phenomenon would it be to be born alone? Yet from this we must not infer that a

Christian is an autonomous person. No, God has not put us on a lonely road. We are born into a family. And when that family happens to be the church of Jesus Christ, it becomes a true expression of the kind of unity that Christ prayed for in John 17: "I in them, and thou in me, that they may be made perfect in one; and that the world may know that thou hast sent me" (v. 23). This is the kind of unity the world can see.

We see this pattern of unity in the Godhead, the Trinity. In many funerals the readings most always include John 14: "In my Father's house are many mansions: if it were not so, I would have told you. I go to prepare a place for you . . . that where I am, there ye may be also" (vv. 2,3). While this may be legitimately applied to heaven in the future, we see this only as a secondary meaning. In examination of the context, Jesus is talking about the Trinity, how he (Christ) is in the Father and the Father in him. "I am going to be in you," he explains, "and you are going to be in me, and we are going to come and take up our abode with you." In other words, Jesus is saying that he is going to make it possible for us to have a place in the Godhead, to be incorporated into God himself (not, of course, in the same indivisible and distinctive sense in which the Trinity is one). What is intended, undoubtedly, is the primary union by which our human spirit and the divine Spirit become one. This is a vital living unity of those who are welded together into the indissoluable amalgamation of Christ's love.

With our human tendencies for unbalanced views and our sleight of hand by which we manipulate doctrines, we are led to become so taken up with components that we arrive at no sum. Often we mistake contrasts in the Christian faith for contradictions, forgetting that truths about the Truth contrast in order to complement. And so to arrive at the unity of the faith we must drop our *divergencies* while we keep our *diversities*, realizing that we are not fighting one another but often have our backs to one another fighting in opposite directions.

The truth is that we belong to one another. We may vex one another at times. But that is only the more reason we need to see the unity in diversity which God has designed for his church.

We are placed in one Body and at times are called upon to "forbear one another in love." Transcendent grace is given us in Christ for this. All personalities will not chime together in harmonious agreement. Said the late Dr. Joseph Owen: "There are some folks I love so well that I would rather pay their board bill than to live with them." But the love into which we have been sealed in the Body is sufficient to make us accepted in the Beloved and to accept others, even as we ourselves have been accepted. "Wherefore receive ye one another, as Christ also received us to the glory of God" (Rom. 15:7).

The Divine Initiative

Out of this common faith there emerges a common doctrine: keeping the unity of the Spirit. (Note Eph. 4:3.) This is something that the Spirit of God has already achieved. He accomplished it in the morning of our regeneration, when we awakened to discover that we were one with Christ and also one with everyone else who is in Christ. But the unity of the Spirit leads us in verse 13 to the "unity of the faith." When we come into the unity of the faith we are no longer "tossed to and fro and carried away by every wind of doctrine." Notice the distinction between the "wind of doctrine" and the "unity of the faith." Let us be reminded that it is not doctrine that divides us, it is the "winds of doctrine," doctrine that shifts from one generation to another, from one era to another. Seminaries often wear new styles of theology that are as ephemeral as they are seasonal. Just think of the "winds of doctrine" that have blown through the church's age, from first-century gnosticism (which I John is countering) to twentieth-century existentialism. All of them are "isms" which tomorrow will become "wasms."

And all of this happens because the immature children who have not grown up in Christ insist on their partialism. It may be a partial concern for man's soul with no regard for his body; it may be an undue emphasis on the healing of the body with no regard for those "psychic slivers" that infest the human mind. It may be an overemphasis on eschatology by which we alienate large segments of the church, because they don't see through our particular lens and fit into our closed categories.

A daughter who was seeking so desperately to be understood by her mother, said to her painfully one day, "O Mother, just look at me once, as though you really see me!" When we find church members who are taken up with the arc and are ignoring the circle, fascinated by the sparks and are forgetting the flame, we want to cry out, "Will you please look at the church for once as if you really did see it!" Do you perceive what the church is when the church functions in its pristine purity?

> Love, like death, hath all destroyed,
> Rendered all distinctions void:
> Names and sects and parties fall:
> Thou, O Christ, art all in all.   (Charles Wesley)

The middle partition wall has been broken down.

One of the most beautiful examples of this unity in diversity is a symphony orchestra. The Greek word for "agree" is symphony. Jesus said, "Where two or three agree on earth, as touching one thing, it shall be given them of my Father." When a group of people are in agreement with God and one another, we have a beautiful symphony. The individual members of a symphony orchestra do not copy one another. Rather, each plays his or her own distinctive part. What is it then in an orchestra which unites them? It is the willing submission to the control of one conductor, the subordination to the printed score before them, and the attunement of the inner ear to the total harmony of the whole.

A few weeks ago I heard the North Carolina Symphony Orchestra in concert. Again I was intrigued by the fellow who was standing in the back striking the little triangle. He sat there and every now and again jumped up and "pinged."

I was reminded by a musician friend that if the percussionist didn't "ping" at the right time there would be a very poor performance. And if suddenly he were to jump and say, "I'm going to 'ping' 'til my heart's content," one can imagine the results. God's church is orchestrated. Following the deft baton of the Great Conductor, the Holy Spirit, every member plays his part. But if one member ceases to function or overfunctions, there is a cacophony. When the human body is orchestrated we call that health. It is a well-tuned body. Paul spoke to the Corinthians of those who were weak and sick and sleeping, because they did not discern the Lord's body in their communion (I Cor. 11:30).

When we do not discern the Lord's Body we are cut off from our spiritual supply. It is the total body that gives strength to any one member of that body. The Ephesian epistle presents a Christ-whelmed and joy-filled people whose tuneful souls declare to the world that God, the Holy Spirit, is conducting. And the body members blend into a symphony whose rapturous harmonies resound the triumph of heaven's glorious King.

The Unifying Person

Years ago, David mused on the human body and said it was "fearfully and wonderfully made." What an amazing unity of diversity, with its intricately convoluted brain which centers its communication system, its complex circuitry of nerves, its compound chemical balance, its muscular flexibility, all of which finds its counterpart in the church. Paul refers to it as "a glorious church." And no wonder. When a thing answers to the satisfaction of God, it is glorious. All that God has planned is calculated to be to "the praise of his glory" (Eph. 1:12).

The Pattern

An Old Testament reflection of this in pattern form is found in the creation of the tabernacle in the wilderness. It was meticulously prescribed down to a detail, to a pin, to a thread, to a color, to a measure. And we read, "As the Lord had commanded Moses," "as the Lord had commanded Moses." It is a recurrent phrase.

When things answered to God's design, fulfilling his nature and mind, when he was satisfied, delighted, and well pleased, there came back something of his own satisfaction in reflection. And that was glorious. When God looked upon his Son, the Lord Jesus Christ, at his baptism, God spoke out of his excellency, saying, "This is my beloved Son in whom I am well pleased." "And we beheld his glory, the glory of the only begotten Son of the Father, full of grace and truth." Glory is the rebound of God's complete satisfaction. When things answer to the nature of God, that's glorious.

In the Genesis account, we read that when God had

finished his creation and everything was as he had intended and commanded, he declared, "And it was so, and so it was, and so it was as the Lord commanded." "And God saw every thing that he had made, and, behold, it was very good" (Gen. 1:31).

What an experience it must have been to have lived in the atmosphere of that glorious morning of creation, in a realm where everything satisfied God and where there was the sense of his complete satisfaction and pleasure. Such complete agreement between heaven and earth produces a symphony. This is the reason the book of Ephesians has a lyrical tone.

Listen to these great phrases from Ephesians: "Now unto him that is able to do exceeding abundantly above all that we ask or think, according to the power that worketh in us, unto him be glory in the church by Christ Jesus throughout all ages, world without end" (3:20-21). "Speaking to yourselves in psalms and hymns and spiritual songs, singing and making melody in your heart" (5:19). It sings itself into your soul.

I believe this whole universe has a musical tone and that all the planets reflect God's glory and praise, perhaps all except this earth of ours. God is wanting to end the rift so that there will be a symphony, an agreement again. Job said, "In the morning of creation the stars sang together and the sons of God shouted for joy." That is glory!

When we obey God's commandments and are committed to his lordship, always and ever we will find a glorious life. In Ephesians 1:9-11 we read: "Having made known unto us the mystery of his will, according to his good pleasure which he hath purposed in himself: that in the dispensation of the fulness of times he might gather together in one all things in Christ, both which are in heaven, and which are on earth; even in him: in whom also we have obtained an inheritance, being predestinated according to the purpose of him who worketh all things after the counsel of his own will." What is the counsel of his own will? "That we should be the praise of his glory, who first trusted in Christ" (1:12). That is, we should be so constituted as a people of God that, constantly, others would be praising God, because of us.

Whether it is a building, a bride, or a body (Paul uses all three appellations concerning the church), when it answers to the perfect satisfaction of heaven, the result is always glorious.

That is the reason for the joy of birth. God in his infinite artistry weaves an embryo in such a delicate and incredible manner that one set of cells becomes a thinking organism, while another set produces coronary arteries so perfectly joined to the entire system that life is carried to every part by the blood, another set of cells results in a vascular system, and so on. We can only glorify God for this marvelous creation.

It is a superlative delight to know that we shall not lose these bodies. All of us want to be more than "good ghosts" in some ethereal sphere. We long to have these bodies restored. The redemption in Christ includes the resurrection of the body. We will have the same body, but the body will not be the same. Paul speaks of "being clothed upon" with a body from on high, a new body fashioned after Christ's own glorious one. Someone asked me recently, "Do you think we are going to recognize one another in heaven?" I quoted Brother Rufus Mosely who said, "I bought a new suit of clothes, and when I put on the coat that had never been worn before, I hadn't had it on five minutes before it took on the Moseley look." When we are clothed in immortality, God is not going to erase our identity to destroy our personality. He is going to release, enhance, and magnify it. The body is a wonderful thing, because God thought of it. Don't ever minimize it. It's to be presented to him as a living sacrifice. If it is not presented to God it will be a confused bundle of complexes and nerves as we project our inner disunity to the outside world.

Fallen man, under the stroke of what the theologians call original sin, is not to be despised. Though fallen, man is not like a hovel in the back alley. He is more like a cathedral that has been struck by a bomb. The second and third levels have been shattered and have mingled with the first level, and the building has become a confused rubble. The fall confused the hierarchical system of spirit, soul, and body. They were no longer in their proper ascendency. But even so, all the suggestiveness of original splendor is there. How glorious is the unity of the human body when the members are rightly related to one another and to the head.

The Person

There are seven members of this unity of faith. (See Ephesians 4:4-6: Paul speaks of God's purpose to gather all this together and to prepare a body that will reflect his glory so that the world will see that glory and believe. That was Jesus' prayer in John 17. It's not simply our doctrine that is going to convince the world; it's the glory.) Three of these are persons of the Godhead. Note the order:

One Body, One Spirit, One Hope
One Lord
One Faith, One Baptism, One God and Father of all.

It is interesting that the apostle, in speaking of this unity, puts the Lord Jesus in the center. The centrality of the Jesus Christ is evident throughout the scripture. God's invincible determination is that he should become in the heart realm what he is already in the heavenly realm, both Lord and Christ.

The truth about the church is that Jesus is its exalted head. In Colossians, Christ is presented as the head, in Ephesians the church as the Body, and in Corinthians, individual Christians as members. Jesus as Lord is the truth about the church.

Jesus as Lord is the *truth about our hope*. What is that hope? It is the blessed hope of the unveiling of Jesus as Lord so that every knee will bow and every tongue confess that he is Lord to the glory of God. He will be manifested as King of kings and Lord of lords, and we are the kings over which he is King. For "they which receive abundance of grace and of the gift of righteousness shall reign in life by one, Jesus Christ" (Rom. 5:17).

The *truth is that justifying faith* has as its object the Lord Jesus Christ. "Therefore being justified by faith, we have peace with God through our Lord Jesus Christ." It is not the volume of faith that saves us. Often, people say to me, "I need more faith." We don't. We are just oozing with the stuff all the time. We use it every minute of the day. It is not the quantity but the object of our faith that saves us.

Christ alone is the object of our faith. He is the express image of the Father. No man has seen God at any time. God is a spirit. "They that worship him must worship him in spirit and truth." Jesus did not come to this earth to be God—he came to be man, telling the truth about God. "Though He was never ever less than God, He was never ever more than man," says Ian Thomas.

The *truth about baptism* is that we are baptized into a body of which he is the Lord, and we are made to drink of his Spirit. The human spirit is infused with the divine spirit but never loses its identity; the human ego is not destroyed, it is simply cleansed of its inordinate egoism. The primary meaning of the word *baptism* is "plunge" or "immerse." In any language there is a literal and metaphorical meaning of a word. We must be careful with analogies. As C. S. Lewis has reminded us, when Jesus suggested that we are to be "wise as serpents and harmless as doves," he did not imply that we were to lay eggs! Likewise, water is not the element but rather the metaphor for baptism. The Holy Spirit is the substance of which water is the shadow or symbol.

I am not depreciating the emphasis today on the fullness of the Holy Spirit in our experience. It is not an option, for we are to be filled with the Spirit. To be less than filled is to be less than fit for the purposes of God. But to use the phrase *the baptism* without definition is ill-advised. Baptism is our position in Christ; filling is our possession. As God invades our lives by the presence of the Holy Spirit, he elevates Jesus as Lord. He puts him on the throne of our lives. Here, Christ picks up the scepter of his sovereignty, sweeps our human personalities with his benign theocracy, and we become filled with the fullness of God. Our minds are filled with his thoughts, our natures with his love, and our tongues with his praise. Baptism is an act. Filling is an action. Filling is not a second blessing, it is the second part of the first blessing.

In classical Greek drama a drunken slave is told by another that he is "baptized." Obviously what *baptized* means is that he has been taken over by another force that has captivated his personality and put it under tribute to the invading element. In Christian baptism that element is the Holy Spirit, the other self of our risen Lord of glory. He makes us one with the nature of God. "For both he that sanctifieth and they who are sanctified are all of one: for which cause he is not ashamed to call them brethren" (Heb. 2:11).

Christ is not ashamed of us, because we bear his nature. We are given a place in the person of God. "I go to prepare a place for you," said Jesus in John 14:2. The entire chapter has to do with his oneness with the Father. "At that day ye shall know that I am in my Father, and ye in me, and I in you" (v. 20). Jesus prepared for his disciples a place in the very nature of God himself.

It is not death but baptism which fulfills Christ's promise of John 14. For heaven is not what God makes, heaven is what God is. And when God is manifest, that is heaven. I do not mean that there is not a literal heaven. I believe there is a place God has prepared where we shall enter and be with the Lord forever. We read in Hebrews 9:24: "For Christ is not entered into the holy places made with hands, which are the figures of the true; but into heaven itself, now to appear in the presence of God for us." But what makes heaven heaven? Surely not the pearly gates or golden streets or jasper walls or multithroated celestial choirs. What makes heaven heaven is the Lamb on the throne. And what makes heaven on earth is the same thing, that is, the Lamb on the throne of the human heart.

There is a man whose wife had six major surgical operations. A few months ago she had a hemorrhage and because of the loss of blood she was rushed to the hospital with very little pulse. Her husband was immediately at her side in the emergency room. In this desperate moment he remembered his confession. He knew instinctively that Christ was reigning. In that mystical moment there came to him the scriptural injunction: "Be still and know that I am God." (God always is on an "I am" basis.) Suddenly there came to him the overwhelming sense that God was in that place, spreading his peace. It was the following day that this man came buoyantly into my study. He said to me, "Something wonderful has happened. You've got to tell it. Everybody must know it. I know it. My brain knows it. My heart knows it. Every fiber of my being is aware of it. Jesus is alive!" And then describing the aforementioned event, he said, "In that moment of illumination I knew there was no sickness and no death in him. He fills everything! Death cannot prevail in God's holy presence. In that moment, nothing mattered but God!"

I then reflected on something Dr. Joseph Haroutounian once said, "To be free is to live and die so that anxiety is overruled by faith."

Here is a heart baptized in the consciousness of God. The Lamb is on the throne. Heaven is a present condition. As Samuel Rutherford, the Scottish covenanter, exclaimed while in prison, "Jesus Christ entered my cell last evening and every stone became alive with beauty!"

God had prepared a place for himself in Rutherford's heart as he had in my friend's heart that memorable night. Wherever Jesus reigns, blessings abound!

We see this in the book of Revelation. The Christians under persecution were singing their triumphant songs *now*. You would have expected them to be singing the hallelujah chorus in heaven. But they were singing as the mailed fist of atrocity was smashing against them. Nero, Domitian, Diocletian, all in satanic fury, were turning rivers red with martyrs' blood. Yet these Christians were riding each wave of persecution with the triumph song: "Amen, hallelujah, the Lord God omnipotent reigneth." The church is more united in warfare than in peace. John caught this beatific vision of the saints' worshiping in heaven and brought it back to earth.

> Some day or other I shall surely come
> Where true hearts wait for me;
> Then let me learn the language of that home
> While here on earth I be:
> Lest my poor lips for want of words be dumb
> In that high company.   (James Stewart, *The Wind of the Spirit* [1968] Nashville: Abingdon Apex ed., 1975.)

The Preeminence

It is the power of the Holy Spirit making Jesus' lordship real that produces unity. Our divisiveness in the church stems from the fact that we have not been rightly related to our exalted Head.

If we were to take twelve balls, place them on a table, and attempt to bring them together, how would we do it? We could attempt to push them together horizontally, but this would only scatter them. But attach a string to each ball, then take those string ends as they converge at the center point in the hand, and slowly begin to lift them. By the very law of physics they will huddle together in a fraternal formation.

The oneness of heart that is the purpose of God for his people is achieved by the Holy Spirit who lifts our affection to things above where Christ sits at the right hand of God. He begins to stretch our souls toward sanctity and gravitate our hearts toward holiness, the impulse of which is in the very heart of the Trinity.

That is the purpose of the baptism of the Holy Spirit. Our theological pluralism ends where the lordship of Christ begins. Our divisiveness ends, because we are drawn together by the lordship of Jesus Christ.

There was a professor in a certain divinity school who took delight in shocking the students with his blatant negations. When speaking in chapel one day he was casting doubtful reflections on the virgin birth of Christ. At that particular time a spiritual mentor of mine, Rufus Moseley, was in the school doing research. He heard this professor, and his spirit was disturbed. He went to him and said, "I understand that you do not believe that Jesus Christ was born of a Virgin. The professor began to remonstrate, as he cited classical interpretations. Brother Rufus very gently said, "There seems to be a bit of controversy here. I want to know if you have ever bowed your knee before the Lord Jesus and asked him whether he was born of a virgin?" The professor confessed that he had not. Brother Rufus suggested that together they end this controversy by bowing in prayer and asking Jesus about it. After both had prayed, the professor (who obviously had received no illumination at this point) wanted to know what the Lord had said. Brother Rufus answered, "The Lord Jesus said to me, 'Yes, Rufus, I was born of a Virgin, but be as kind as you can to those who haven't seen it yet!' "

Our theological pluralism is simply an expression of the repudiation of Christ's lordship. I am not speaking of our theological diversity. That is a thing of beauty. Each member is able to express his distinctiveness while complementing the whole Body of Christ. Its counterpart is the human body. When I arise in the morning to begin my day, it is not my hands that begin to dictate to the head what they plan to do. Every part of my body functions differently, but all parts are so related to the head that they work in harmony. No part of my body is jealous of another part. My eye does not say to my ear, "This is my territory. Get off!" If a wasp is about to sting my ear, my hand fights for my ear. This is possible only because of a single headship to which the body gladly submits.

There is a lot of talk about Christianity's being one of the major religions of the world. But these religions are basically organized efforts on the part of individuals to achieve their salvation by following the teachings of a dead prophet. They seek merit and peace in an afterlife. One Eastern religion, for example, teaches that our good deeds will merit a higher reincarnation, and one could conceivably go on being reincarnated until one reaches a state of perfection in which nirvana is achieved. Nirvana is that passionless state of imperturbability where nothingness prevails. Isn't that a blessed hope! Extinguishment, not fulfillment, is the end.

The Christian faith is set in contradistinction to this kind of philosophy. It is not based upon the life of a dead prophet. Ours is the only solitary figure of all human history who walked away from the tomb to world conquest and is alive now, guiding cosmic forces and thrusting life toward the kingdom of God.

There came only one man who went into the deep arcana of death, broke the last darkness of this universe, rose again, neatly folded his graveclothes, and laid them aside to walk away from a graveyard, showing himself alive by many infallible proofs. We must never include Christianity among the comparative religions of the world. We have a Christ who is august, unique, supreme, unrivaled, peerless, who is "far above all principality, and power, and might, and dominion, and every name that is named, not only in this world, but also in that which is to come," God himself, dying to destroy death and rising to restore life.

One Lord is the basis of our unity. There is a graphic illustration of this in I Samuel 5. The Philistines had confiscated the sacred ark of the covenant. This represented the enthronement of God in the life of the nation. The Philistines put this ark in their temple. This temple was dedicated to Dagon, the fish god of the Philistines. (There is always something fishy about a religious pluralism.) The Philistines were superstitious enough to want to regard that ark as an object of veneration. They did not want to deny the validity of Israel's religion. They just didn't want to make it sovereign.

After having put the ark in the temple, they awakened next morning to discover that Dagon had fallen down and was on its face, broken to pieces. Imagine having a god with no head with which to think and no arms with which to lift!

The Lord Jesus always challenges the reign of any other god in your life and mine. "He will overturn, overturn, overturn, until he comes, whose right it is to reign," says Ezekiel. There is in every human heart a Dagon that challenges the lordship of Christ.

There can be no bond of peace and no unity of the Spirit until this matter is settled in our hearts. Where will we bow the knee? Who will ultimately command us? Everything will be overturned until he whose right it is to reign picks up the scepter of his sovereign love and sweeps the horizons of our hearts with his beneficent rule.

What makes the church the Church is that each individual member has bowed the knee at Christ's feet, acknowledging his right to reign.

Everything will be in disarray in our lives and in our world until he is again acknowledged as the integrating center by which life is united.

The Unifying Perspective

The entire New Testament perspective seems to be brought into focus in Ephesians 4:6, "One God and Father of all, who is above all, and through all, and in you all."

Paul links the doctrine of unity with that of the Holy Trinity. The Trinity is the *pattern* for our unity. But it is also the *pledge* of our oneness. For the ascended Lord Jesus, in unison with the Father, confers the Holy Spirit upon his church. The unity of the Holy Spirit's baptism is the bond of our peace (Eph. 4:3).

There are seven members of this unity, with the Lord Jesus Christ in the center, as we have already observed. But while there are three persons, there is one God and Father of us all, "who is above all, and through all, and in you all."

This brings us up against the doctrine of the immanence of God. It is critical that we understand this in contrast with the pantheism of Eastern religions. Pantheism teaches that God is in everything—"God oozing out of the acorns." The pantheist sees a tree and worships it, because God is in it. When this thought-form is followed, we would have to conclude that since God is in everything, even the devil is filled. No! That is not what we have here. It is not God in everything but everything in God. "In him we live, and move, and have our being" (Acts 17:28).

There is a big difference between some transcendental "total awareness or consciousness" and the truth we face here. God chooses where he pours out his Spirit or withdraws himself.

So let us examine the propositions set forth in this passage:

Possession: "One God and Father of all."

"One God and Father of all." That's possession. "All things come of thee, O Lord, and of thine own have we given thee." He is the Author of life, the Creator of the world. "All things were made by him." "In the beginning was the Word, and the Word was with God, and the Word was God."

To the Hebrew mind the word was a communication of an invisible idea. We don't think words are too significant in our culture. We hear inanities churned out all day long on TV talk shows. In Hebrew thought, words brought something into existence that could never be annihilated. For example, if I spoke an evil against someone and subsequently met that person, that word I had spoken would be hanging there between us and our relationship. It was by the Word that this world was created. To the Greek mind the Word meant the idea behind the universe, the reason behind existence.

The combined thought is that God both invented the world and had a purpose behind the invention. He made it to function according to divine laws. And since it all came from him he has a better idea of how it should run than all the surmisings of men. One reason God hates sin is that it won't work. It frustrates rather than fulfills life.

"All things are of him." This world came from him. If that be true, did God make atom bombs, hand grenades, and hallucinogenic drugs?

No! God made atoms, but man made atom bombs. God made plants, but men made strange chemical formulations that take over the control tower of the human brain and prostitute man's self-image. Everything that came from God was good. He pronounced it to be so in the morning of creation. But man failed to follow divine wisdom in developing and utilizing the natural resources.

Yet all things are of him. This is a basic philosophy that governs all human behavior. For if there is no God from which we came, then there is no God to whom we return. If there is no God to whom we return then we have no judge. If we have no judge, then we have no moral responsibility. If we have no moral responsiblity, then our actions have no consequence. And if our actions are inconsequential, then value goes and life turns pale. "When God goes, goal goes. When goal goes, value goes. And when value goes, life turns dead on our hands," wrote E. Stanley Jones. We are motivated in our country today by a philosophy that is conducive to the delusion of man's self-redemption, the myth that man can be man apart from God.

Some time ago I was sitting next to a Buddhist on a plane. We attempted to examine the distinctiveness of the Christian faith over against the religious system of Buddhism. In the course of conversation I made the statement that Jesus Christ was God's absolute among all the relativisms of life. "But there are no absolutes!" he protested. "Haven't you read Einstein's theory of relativity?"

I have learned to give one answer to such an asseveration of nonfaith. When one affirms, "There are no absolutes," my answer is, "Are you absolutely sure?"

We cannot live without absolutes. What kind of world would it be if everybody kept his own brand of time with no reference to Greenwich mean time? And where do we get this prime basis of standard time? It is from the heavens where God has set something so absolute that it can be depended upon year in and year out.

In the philosophically delightful book *The East, No Exit*, Os Guinness has a chapter entitled "Dust of Death" in which he emphasizes the fact that without objective reality (absolutes) we lose our civilization.

Without the absolute authority of Jesus Christ, the one God who created heaven and earth, we finally cannot distinguish between *reality* and *fantasy*. As Lao-tse, the Chinese philosopher who is supposed to be the founder of Taoism, 604 B.C, put it: "If, when I was asleep I was a man dreaming I was a butterfly, how do I know when I am awake I am not a butterfly dreaming I am a man?"

This may mean little to some of us, but to those who have lost their grip on reality through carelessly applied meditation techniques or through repeated drug trips, the inability to distinguish between fantasy and reality can become a living hell.

There are many who are asking if the world is not a delusion or a maya. The twentieth-century leader who is the ex-president philosopher of India, Dr. Radakrishnan, a brilliant advocate of sycretism, says that man is "God's temporary self-forgetfulness" (Os Guinness, The East, No Exit). We are God's dream. The true self is God and the "I" which I consider myself to be is really the "non-self" caught in the world of illusion, bondage, and ignorance.

Alan Watts likens the moral situation to a play. On stage the audience sees the "good man" fighting the "bad man," although everyone knows that backstage the actors are the best of friends. Only in the world of illusion does one believe in good and evil as real and distinct. Backstage, God and Satan are the best of friends. Thus the ideal is to get backstage into transcendent consciousness so that one is beyond the distinctions of good and evil.

This kind of fuzzed thinking, feathered with pessimism, has a profound effect upon the social progress of our race. Jerome Tuccille excoriates such a philosophical delusion in the following analysis:

We have accepted the basic premise of those who would undermine our free enterprise system all over the world, and instead of refuting their arguments with logical convictions based on the Word of God which are the only sound philosophical presuppositions, we proceed to apologize for our wealth and explain that we really are getting more progressive every day and intend to share our prosperity with the underprivileged of the world.

When we are told that millions are starving in India while we "selfishly" enjoy our automobiles, refrigerators, private homes, and other luxuries, what do we reply? Do we say that these people are victims of a crippling religious heritage that can be traced back to the Stone Age, a philosophical tradition that teaches them to hate the world and withdraw from it, and that starvation is the logical end of such a heritage? We do not. We accept the premises of our accusers, apologize for our prosperity as if it were at the expense of those who are going hungry, and export tons of food instead of ideas which are most urgently required. ("Re-Examining Our Convictions," *Applied Christianity*, February, 1973, pp. 40-41)

Oppenheimer, a leading nuclear scientist, observed that there would be no technological advances as we know them in the Western world if it were not for Christian mentality. What he was saying is that the heavens are so absolute that we can calculate with unerring accuracy the landing of a rocket on the moon, because of these fixed, immutable laws of the universe.

A friend tells about being in Tokyo in 1960, where he witnessed an unusual court scene. A man was on trial for running through a red light and colliding with another auto. The driver who violated the traffic rules on the red light was fined 75 percent of the cost of court. The man who had passed through the green light with no violation was nevertheless fined 25 percent of costs. We would say one was wrong and the other was right. But that's because of our concept of an absolute God. The Japanese court ruled that there would have been no accident if the man who went through the green light had not been there. Thus we see how relativism affects even our jurisprudence, leaving us with no categories of right and wrong.

The greatness of Britain and America is that our laws find their reflection in the Word of God. Even the technological advances of countries such as Japan have had the import of Western systems of thought.

Western thought has been derived from this assumption: "One God the Father of all . . ." "Thus saith God the Lord, he that created the heavens, and stretcheth them out; he that spread forth the earth, and that which cometh out of it; he that giveth breath unto the people upon it, and spirit to them that walk therein" (Isa. 42:5).

Ours is the creative God. All things belong to him. By his act of creation the human race came into being. If we lay hold of this truth we shall have a basic premise by which we as mere creatures can claim a place in the sovereign will of a purposeful God.

"In the beginning God ..." Starting with this basic life assumption we have an exciting world view. It opens up for us a world of miraculous potential.

The story goes that Sir Isaac Newton needed a cat for his barn. His neighbor offered him a cat if he would also take the litter of kittens. Sir Isaac made one large hole for the cat and several small holes for the kittens (as if they all couldn't get through the cat hole). Genesis 1 is our "cat hole." Introduce the universe as having its beginning in God's spontaneous will and its reality in a conferred one which is always relative to his absolute and upholding Word, and we have a safe universe. Evil is derived, not inherent. God is able to perform that which his love and will indicate.

This is the reason for the satanic attack on the books of Genesis and Revelation. In the former, the sentence of defeat and eviction has been pronounced on the devil. In the latter, that sentence is executed.

The modern objection to the Christian understanding of creation has been raised at the point of the relation of creation to time. Whether time was created along with the universe is a moot question. It is useless to attempt to assess it. It is fully useful however to declare that Christ is the Lord of time. How old was the wine when Jesus created it at Cana of Galilee? How big were the trees in Eden when he created them? God does not have to wait for anything to age, not wine or anything else. He can create fossils if he wishes, just to throw atheistic researchers off the trail and confound the wisdom of the wise. The fact is irrevocable and indisputable. "One God and Father of all"

Father of all denotes possession. This is God's world. He made it by Jesus Christ and for him. Its predestination is that of a Christian planet. The mind and will of God is not merely stamped on this creation as an afterthought. It is plowed into it in furrows so deep that neither French Revolutionist nor Marxist Communist nor German humanist nor American secularist can cover it over.

Protection: "One God . . . who is above all." ⫣

"One God and Father of all who is *above* all." That is *protection*. He presides over his universe. "What fools the nations are to rage against the Lord! How strange that men should try to outwit God! For a summit conference of the nations has been called to plot against the Lord and his Messiah, Christ the King" (Ps. 2:1-2 TLB). But God has set upon his holy hill of Zion his beloved Son.

> The light that shines from Zion's Hill
>   Shall lighten every land;
> The King that reigns from Salem's tower
>   Shall all the world command.   (Michael Bruce)

It is not that he *shall* reign. He *does* reign. History is his story, from first to last—from Capitol Hill to Cambodia, from Berlin to Johannesburg, from near East to far West. "One God, one law, one element / And one far-off divine event, / To which the whole creation moves" (Tennyson).

We do not sit passively before inevitable recurring cycles of trouble. This universe is moving toward a goal; God is presiding. John Calvin was asked to modify his concept of the sovereignty of God to say that "God's eye was over history." "Not so," said Calvin. "God's hand is on history." The sovereignty of God is his hand in the glove of history. Everything that is over our head is under his feet. This is not pious prattle but an irrevocable fact.

Just as there were periodic earthly convocations when God required Israel to assemble at Jerusalem to keep the feasts of the Lord recorded in the book of Leviticus, the Bible points to periodic convocations when all spirits are summoned before the Most High to give an account of their stewardship. The book of Job indicates this is the case. Satan appeared before the throne of God with the sons of men. In I Kings we read:

And the Lord said, Who shall persuade Ahab, that he may go up and fall at Ramoth-gilead? And one said on this manner, and another said on that manner. And there came forth a spirit, and stood before the Lord, and said, I will persuade him. And the Lord said unto him, Wherewith? And he said, I will go forth, and I will be a lying spirit in the mouth of all his prophets. (22:20-22)

All created spirits are ruled over by the sovereign God who is "above all."

When Christ ascended from Mount Olivet, carrying to the highest heights of heaven that incarnate body, scarred with the marks of our eternal redemption, God set him at his own right hand, "far above all principalities and powers." And today he rules the revolutionary forces by the hidden wisdom of his Cross. "Surely the wrath of man shall praise thee: the remainder of wrath shalt thou restrain" (Ps. 76:10).

Here is a perceptive word from the late A. W. Tozer:

God sovereignly decreed that man should be free to exercise moral choice, and man from the beginning has fulfilled that decree by making his choice between good and evil. When he chooses to do evil, he does not thereby countervail the sovereign will of God but fulfills it, inasmuch as the eternal decree decided not which choice the man should make but that he should be free to make it. If in His absolute freedom God has willed to give man limited freedom, who is there to stay His hand or say, "What doest thou?" Man's will is free because God is sovereign. A God less than sovereign would not bestow moral freedom upon His creatures. He would be afraid to do so. (The Knowledge of the Holy, New York: Harper & Row, p. 117)

But to those who recognize this sovereign right of God to rule in equity through Jesus Christ are those who comprise his church, which is his Body. One man who responds to that sovereignty at any time in history can make a difference. *History can act on the faith of the uncommitted, but the faith of the committed acts on history.* Abraham in Canaan, Joseph in prison, Moses in Egypt, Elijah on Carmel, Mordecai in Persia, Paul and Silas in Philippi, Dorcas in Joppa, Titas on Crete, and John on Patmos are examples of the sovereignty of God working through the free will of man and overruling and overturning the counsels of nations. "My counsel shall stand," saith the Lord (Isa. 46:10).

Purpose: "Through All"

"One God and Father of all, who is above all, and through all." That's purpose. God works through all circumstances to his ends. "He worketh all things after the counsel of his own will."

I love the lines of the Word of God: "The evening and the morning were the first day." That is the theme of the whole Bible. The message of the Bible is that God is always working through darkness to light, through chaos to order, through weakness to strength, through cursing to blessing.

Paul was aware of this when he wrote in the first verse of chapter four: "I therefore, the prisoner of the Lord" (Eph.). Paul had his eye single. It was Caesar who had him in jail, but he would not take his imprisonment from the Roman emperor. And where did he learn this? From the Lord Jesus Christ. In the Garden, Jesus prayed, "Let this cup pass from me. Nevertheless, not my will but thine be done." Rising from that prayer he said to Peter, "Put your sword back into the sheath, for the cup *which my Father giveth me,* shall I not drink it." But were we informed that Annas, Caiaphas, Judas, and the whole motley crowd mixed the contents of that cup? "No, I won't take it from them, I'll only take it from my Father," Jesus was saying.

When Paul wrote the Ephesian letter he was in Rome, dwelling in a rented house with special privileges as a Roman citizen. But he was chained to a Praetorian Guard. (They were the select young men of the empire who surrounded the emperor.) If Paul had to be chained to the guard, it meant that the guard had to be chained to Paul. (These men changed shifts every six hours.) Which of these is the prisoner, and for whom should our sympathy extend? May I suggest that the Roman guards were the discomfited. They were trying to live nice, quiet pagan lives. But as guard after another would come on duty and under Paul's preaching, they would bow to the claims of one mightier than the Roman emperor.

The disciples were really worried about Paul's imprisonment. "What is going to happen to the church? Our beloved apostle is in jail," they would surmise. Yet look in the first chapter of Philippians: "But I would ye should understand, brethren, that the things which happened unto me have fallen out rather unto the furtherance of the gospel; so that my bonds in Christ are manifest in all the palace, and in all other places" (vv. 12-13). And in Philippians 4:22: "All the saints salute you, chiefly they that are of Caesar's household." Through Paul's imprisonment, the imperial palace was infiltrated with messengers of Jesus Christ's who were there to unseat Caesar and to enthrone the Savior. It was not long before Caesar's throne had toppled and those Roman roads were the pathways for the immortal tread of God's Evangel.

> In the center of the circle
>   Of the will of God I stand;
> There can be no second causes,
>   All must come from His dear hand.   (Source unknown)

We must be clear in our understanding. We are not to infer that God brings good out of evil. Evil is always evil, never good. It is never good in the making. It is never undeveloped good. Evil is the repudiation of Christ's lordship, the contradiction of the divine will, the patent violation of divine Law. But God so works his sovereign purpose that he antagonizes evil men, vile institutions, and rebellious movements, that in the end they develop the good they intend to destroy.

Power: "In You All"

"One God and Father of all, who is above all, and through all, and in you all." That's power.

God does not give us power. He gets in us and is the power of daily living, the total adequacy of our lives.

> Whatever then He asks of me,
> I know that He Himself must be. (Paraphrase)

The power needed in our lives is of an inward and moral nature. The world thinks of power in terms of political shrewdness, financial security, social prestige, or military prowess. And that kind of power tends to corrupt.

But the power offered by our altogether victorious and adequate Savior is the moral reinforcement for the living of worthy and Christlike lives. This is not power that generates a lot of volatile feeling, catapulting people into an orbit of emotionalism, who will subsequently give the shabbiest type of exhibition of holiness in the home, business, or neighborhood. This is a moral control that enables us to walk worthy of our vocation. "I therefore, the prisoner of the Lord, beseech you that ye walk worthy [connotes fitness] of the vocation wherewith ye are called, with all lowliness and meekness, with longsuffering, forbearing one another in love" (Eph. 4:1-2).

There is an ethical dynamic at the heart of the gospel. Our belief releases the power of the object of our faith which is the life of Christ.

In the first three chapters of Ephesians, Paul is saying, "God did this!" And the whole of it is written in a burst of praise. It is a symphony of what God did in Christ and reaches a crescendo when God raised him from the dead.

Now Paul says, in effect, "Since God has done this, you are to do this." What is my fitting response? It is to "walk . . . in all lowliness and meekness, in longsuffering, forbearing one another in love."

This takes power. Such humility takes nothing less than the power displayed in the coming of the Son of God to earth. "This shall be a sign unto you, you shall find the babe wrapped in swaddling clothes, lying in a manger," Not, mind you, lying in a palace amidst the appointments of royalty. But this shall be a sign of the kind of person God is and of the character of his kingdom.

How unlike the mighty symbols by which the secularists want to guarantee the salvation of the world. How unlike the power symbols by which men seek to lord it over others. Contrast that with the ensigns of the nations—the eagle, the lion, the hammer and sickle.

The distinctive glory of God is not in his power to hold monopolies of wealth, to release megaton ratings, to wield titanic tools of technology, to dazzle with pomp and empty splendor. The thing that distinguishes God from man as nothing else does is his love for men and his willingness to share his life with sinners, even though the Creator, to do so, must come to this world as a creature. So omnipotence is wrapped in swaddling clothes, majesty girds a towel around his loins and stoops to wash the disciples' feet; the ruler of the universe bows under the weight of a rugged cross.

Here is a new kind of power. It is the power of meekness, humility, long-suffering. The empires of man based on pride are out! The world of Herods, Annases, and the rigid Pharisees, the worldly wise who consider themselves to be real, the great broad world of public human opinion impregnated with the research of useless facts, this army of shadows surrounded by glamour and eminence and deceit and duplicity—none of this will survive the ages.

Here then is the essence of power. He is ever the Lord in servant form. Bethlehem is not just a pantomime. This is the nature of God and the truth about the universe. This is the kind of God that runs our world. Therefore it is a safe universe. When we have someone who loves us enough to offer himself as "a lamb slain from the foundation of the world," then we have a heart we can trust. God lives to serve his creation. He came to minister, not to be ministered unto. And the only way we can minister to him is to assume the role of a servant and with a meek, humble, and patient spirit fulfill our high calling.

This lucidates the vocation into which we have been called (Eph. 4:1). Our vocation is to serve those who have no claim on us. We are the true sons of the Father if we live to fulfill the calling of this faith. Here is the proposition: Having the nature and authority of God himself, since we have been born of his seed, we then live to serve others. Our personhood is realized as we live in conscious union with the Person and spontaneously express his character.

No wonder men are scandalized when the gospel is seriously believed and lived. For this is an age of materialism and violence, and people feel threatened by the standards of Jesus. If they don't accumulate possessions and shore up their affluence and defend themselves by force, then they lose their security and feel defensive, naked, and vulnerable.

But here is the true power that operates this universe. It is the power of humility, of self-giving love. This is the power that God gives when he gets in us.

This constitutes for us the unifying perspective. "One God and Father of all, who is above all, and through all and in you all." We need preachments that will not keep demanding a unity or a love which we cannot rise to, but the proclamation of a God, who in Christ and through the Holy Spirit, can produce and compel both.

The Unifying Priorities

The reference to Christ's descent into hell and ascent into heaven has such great cosmic dimensions that we can hardly be expected to get our minds around it. However, we must not get hung up on problems. Let us run quickly to the purpose.

There are two aspects of truth set forth in this passage. The first is Christ's descent into the depths. It was the mighty invasion of Christ into the dark recesses of death that dazzled the unknown with radiant light. Hell felt the tramp of his martial feet as he trod the way of man's retreat.

> See! the heaven its Lord receives,
> Yet He loves the earth He leaves:
> Though returning to His throne,
> Still He calls mankind His own.   (Charles Wesley)

Thus Christ stretched the road of redemption down to the depths of man's separation, a separation characterized by anomie (loss of purpose), anonymity (loss of personhood), alienation (loss of presence). Most scholars agree that the descent our Lord made was for the purpose of lifting the Old Testament righteous into heaven itself. Heretofore they had been in what was called, "Abraham's bosom," a part of Sheol-Hades. But since atonement had been made, a "new and living way" was opened to enter into the holiest, the presence of God himself.

As a result of this warfare, Christ received the spoils of his victory—a host of those whom he had set free from captivity.

What happened in the heavenly realm is confirmed in the heart realm. Jesus Christ descends into the depths of man's sinnerhood, releases many captive thoughts and emotions and aspirations and sets the captured *heart* free.

> He breaks the power of canceled sin,
> He sets the prisoner free. (Charles Wesley, "O for a Thousand Tongues to Sing")

But that is not all. "He led captivity captive." He died to destroy the power of death and rose to restore the power of life. We are too negative in our concepts. A great God has greatly delivered us but has been raised again to greatly commission us. He flushes into our bloodstream a fresh purpose for living.

The Christian lives by a worthy calling (Eph. 4:1). Christ rose to imbue us with a Christ-centered purpose. The very image of the devil in unredeemed man is this: "Not thy will but mine be done." The very center of Christ's image in redeemed man is this: "Not my will but thine be done."

A schoolboy brought home a report card heavy with poor grades. "What have you to say about this?" asked the father. "One thing for sure," the boy replied, "you know I've not been cheating!" That's good but not good enough.

It is not enough to say to God, "Lord, you know I've not been sinning." The only kind of Christian life God recognizes as valid is not that which is negative in that it does not sin; it is the kind that is positive, in which we are implementing the eternal purpose for which we have been redeemed.

When Christ delivered us and then bound us to himself, we are told that he subsequently gave us as gifts to the church. We are simply beating the air ecclesiastically until we are caught up in the thrill of being linked and leagued with Christ in the great vocation. Christians must once again discover that they are individual cells of Christ's body. Cancer has been best described as a cell that thought it didn't matter. Hosts of Christians have never found how much they matter as they become Christ's functioning intermediaries in today's world.

Christ's gifts to the church as set forth in Ephesians 4 are not exhaustive. They are suggestive. They are not definitive. They are provocative. This is God's order of priorities as the church moves out to be the arm of his strength and the tongue of his spirit.

I. "And he gave some, apostles." This represents authority in the church. The apostles were the first-handers. The credential was that "they had seen the Lord" (I Cor. 9:1). They had certain knowledge of his resurrection.

The language of the apostles is: "I know!" They carried an authority that no man could gainsay. What an apostolic dogmatism rang through the tenor of their preachments and their witness. I agree with a friend who says he does not want to hear a preacher who is "skilled in the art of almost saying something"—my friend leaves church and feels he has been to a meal where the only thing served was Cool Whip.

The first priority in the church is to restore to ascendency those leaders who have met the Lord face to face and heart to heart, who have an experience of the living Christ so thrilling and throbbing, who speak with such assurance of personal discovery behind their words that they are passionate practictioners and zestful heralds of the Good News.

We must have first-hand experience to go with our second-hand tradition. As Brother Rufus Moseley has said, "Apostolic succession is true only as we continue in the apostolic success. If he who sits in Peter's chair (leadership) does not have the spirit of Peter, he will peter out."

God has always made the apostle the foundation of the church. First, Jesus, the chief apostle appointed by God himself (Heb. 3:1). Then the twelve apostles appointed by Jesus. After that, those in the New Testament church who were appointed by the Holy Spirit (Acts 14:14; Gal. 1:19).

It is futile for us to banter about the question of whether

there are apostles appointed in the church today. The whole of God's people are apostolic. The foundation of the church rests upon those who have dug beneath the incrustation that form, fear, and fiction have overlaid to a first-hand, vital faith that releases God in self-authenticating reality.

The late Dr. William Sangster, that seraphic minister of Westminster Central Hall, London (who has left us a name so bright and an influence so benign as to give him a place among the great evangelical leaders of all time), has observed that the Scriptures sustain five universals organically related to the apostolic mission:

1. All men need this life.
2. All men may have this life.
3. All men who have this life know that they have it.
4. All men must witness to its possession.
5. All men must press on to perfection.

The following history of Wesleyana explains this foregone summation: In 1736 John Wesley embarked on the *Simmonds*, a not too large vessel for the new colony of America. He was coming for this express purpose: "My chief motive is the hope of saving my own soul. I hope to learn the true sense of the Gospel of Christ by preaching it to the heathen."

The sovereign God of history put his hand in the glove of events that followed. It was timed so that Wesley would travel with twenty-six Moravians and eighty English colonists. As surely as Jonah had a God-sized fish thrown across his path to deter his lostness, a raging storm was whirled across Wesley's pathway, not so much to deter his lostness as to precipitate his salvation. While the storm was raging the Moravians were calmly singing. This accentuated Wesley's apprehension. The Anglican was frightened, while the Moravians had assurance anchored in a rock-certainty of Christ.

Wesley entered into his diary, Sunday 23: ". . . At night I was awakened by the tossing of the ship . . . and plainly showed that I was unfit, for I was unwilling to die."

All God's storms pass when they have accomplished their purpose. And John Wesley sought out the Moravian pastor, Mr. Spangenberg. "I soon found," said Mr. Wesley, "what spirit he was of; and asked his advice with regard to my own conduct."

Spangenberg's first question had apostolic overtures that exposed Wesley's spiritual poverty: "My brother, I must first ask you one or two questions. Have you the witness within yourself? Does the Spirit of God bear witness with your spirit that you are a child of God?" Wesley said, "I was surprised and knew not what to answer." He observed it and asked, "Do you know Jesus Christ?" "I paused," said Wesley, "and replied, 'I know he is the Savior of the world.' " "True, but do you know he has saved you?" inquired Spangenberg. "I answered, 'I hope he has died to save me.' He only added, 'Do you know yourself?' I said, 'I do.' But I fear they were vain words."

That sent Wesley spinning, and his mental machinery was active until he found that basis of certainty for his preaching and living. On May 24, 1738, the Word of God had wrought upon his soul until assurance had come. Today a vast denomination with some 12 million members owes its existence to that question: "Do you know!" Spangenberg was God's apostle, laying foundations upon which God was to raise up a holy people for his name.

II. ". . . and some, prophets." The next priority in the church is that it attend its prophetic ministry. This is foundational to all other ministries. In Ephesians 2:20 we are told that the foundation of the church is laid on the "apostles and prophets." The church is founded not only on the experience of the apostle but on the knowledge of the prophet. Hosea wrote: "My people are destroyed for lack of knowledge" (Hosea 4:6).

This knowledge is not merely academic. One could cite the multiplication table and be stating truth. Academic truth is correspondence to fact. But the prophet's truth is correspondence to God. It is therefore alive, mighty in inspiration, searching in its challenge, tender in its benediction, and holy in its compassion.

The prophet is no answer-man. Often when people come to us with intractable questions we have to point them to Deuteronomy 29:29, "The secret things belong unto the Lord our God; but those things which are revealed belong unto us and to our children forever." It is these revealed matters that concern the prophet. Some unanswered questions and mysteries will have to be carried throughout the broad stretch of the eternities. We will raise our hands like Paul and exclaim, "O the depth of the riches both of the wisdom and knowledge of God! how unsearchable are his judgments, and his ways past finding out! For who hath known the mind of the Lord? or who hath been his counsellor?" (Rom. 11:33-34).

Samuel Taylor Coleridge once said that the most profound utterance he had ever read came from the lips of Ezekiel as he looked over the valley of dry bones as God inquired of him: "Can these bones live?" Coleridge observed that if Ezekiel had said yes he would have been presumptuous. If he had said no he would have been faithless. But instead he looked up to God and said, "O Lord, thou knowest." It was then that the vision came of the church's being revived and assembled in the unity and power of the living Spirit.

The prophet is the one who takes off his shoes in the presence of the mystery of revelation before he thunders in the courts of the kings of this world. His eyes are blazingly filled with the glory of God, his heart is burned clean in the fires of God, and his voice is resonant with the Word of God. The prophetic mind has a way of transcending the immediate and coming to us with a vertical word that cuts right across our baptized prejudices. It is that ministry illuminated by the Holy Spirit which calls God's people to biblical principles and guides them amidst the clutter and confusion of this world's religious Babylon.

The prophetic ministry steps into the religious relativisms of any age with a sure word of prophecy. Herman Melville in *Pierre* writes these words: "In order that we may know time, two things are necessary. First, a standard of absolute time, in fact, Greenwich time, to serve as a point of reference; and secondly, a knowledge of the meridian of longitude on which one happens to be situated."

The prophet is the one who knows the standard of God's perfect will which serves as a point of reference and as a knowledge of the meridian of longitude on which the people happen to be traveling. He knows his God and his age.

Prophetic truth intrudes into daily and private living. It understands the confusion of the human heart and speaks with clarifying wisdom. It reconnoiters the human heart with the piercing light of heaven and surprises the hearer with its discernment of secret thoughts.

Scholars can probe the past; the prophet penetrates the present and assesses the deep needs of the hour. Albert Camus once voiced the condition of men with a bit of autobiographical flash: "I progressed on the surface of life in the realm of words as it were, never in reality."

The church proceeds on the surface of words until the prophet comes. Never have we had so much religious superficiality. Every day we get publicity on new movements, associations, programs, and propaganda of religious activity throughout the nation. We are told that in the state of California alone, a new movement arises every week. One religious leader indicated that the climate there is so mild that they can grow both "fruit and nuts."

In the evangelical world there are unprecedented reports of exotic experiences of a subjective nature. We rejoice to believe that many are authentic confrontations with God the Holy Spirit. But much of it has very little solid spiritual substance. We need the critical eye of the prophet over us.

Consider the incident of Jesus' wanting to wash Peter's feet at the Last Supper. Peter's rejoinder is revealing: "Thou shalt never wash my feet. Jesus answered him, If I wash thee not, thou has no part with me. Simon Peter saith unto him, Lord, not my feet only, but also my hands and my head. Jesus saith to him, He that is washed needeth not save to wash his feet, but is clean every whit: and ye are clean, but not all" (John 13:8-10).

Commenting on this verse Mary Webster said, "Peter *rejected the essential, and sought the unnecessary.*" What a prophetic insight! The prophet is one who can discern, discriminate, and declare what is central and what is periferal.

The church today is busy talking, petitioning, protesting, lobbying, voting, boycotting, writing, marching in order to demonstrate its relevancy until it has become the cheerleader for most any new cause that comes blowing down the pike. This activism assumes all sorts of forms, including quasi spiritual ones.

The prophetic ministry quickly penetrates to the root causes. Remember the city of Jericho in Elijah's time? When Elijah came to the gate of the city he was met by a committee who sought his counsel. "Behold, . . . the situation of this city is pleasant, . . . but the water is bad, and the land is unfruitful" (II Kings 2:19 RSV).

The substance of the report was this: the land was pleasant in surface appearance. The trees were lovely. The buildings were beautiful. The history was marvelous. The commerce was thriving. The economy was booming. There were lovely amenities for any visitor who came through her gates. But when one would taste the water one would immediately become aware of something dreadfully wrong. The city was in great danger. The springs were polluted. Only a miracle could solve their problem.

The prophet got below the surface to the cause. He bade them bring him a new bowl filled with salt. He applied the salt to the source and the stream was purified and new life began to emerge.

We have lovely appointments in our cities today. But something is wrong with the mainstream. The source of healing for the nation is that stream of water that flows out from under the altar of the church. Ezekiel the prophet saw this in his vision. And he saw that this stream was bringing life and productivity wherever it touched the land (Ezek. 47).

Salt was an indispensible commodity in that economy. "And every oblation of thy meat offering shalt thou season with salt" (Lev. 2:13). Salt represents that which checks pollution, decay, and death. It is one of the Old Testament symbols of the Holy Spirit, which in the New Testament is the risen life of the Lord Jesus Christ. Ezra sent the remnant back to restore the temple in Jerusalem, and among all the measured allotment of essentials he gave them "salt without prescribing how much," an unlimited quantity. This represents the illimitable life of Jesus Christ.

We are looking for scapegoats today. A South Carolina mayor, speaking before a banquet group, observed that there were at least four factors in our social life that we have flailed as causes of our moral breakdown in America. First, we say it is the uneducated. If men knew better they would do better. Second, there are the politicians. If only we could bring them around to honesty. And those minority dissidents—they constitute such a big slice of the problem. If it is not the uneducated, the politicians, or the minorities, then it is the longhaired young people. Said the mayor:

But have you noticed that among the original seventeen indicted in the Watergate Conspiracy not a one was uneducated. In fact, they attended the best schools in the country. There were no blacks or other minorities represented. None of them were politicians. To the contrary, they hadn't even run for a public office, so much as alderman or dogcatcher. And everyone of them had a haircut!

We censure government, politics, the drug traffic, the Mafia, the economy, the Arabs, the Israelis, and on and on we go, affixing blame for our polluted and decadent condition. But when the greatest of all prophets came to the city, instead of excoriating the crowds outside, He went to the heart of the problem and cleansed the temple.

We can never blame the world for acting like the world. The church is set in the midst of the world for a leavening influence. When the church is obedient to our Lord's commands wonderful things happen. "I pray not for the world," said Jesus in John 17. When the church is experiencing the glory of God for which Jesus prayed, the world will be subdued.

Consider the marriage at Cana of Galilee. The wedding had run out of wine. Just think of how many marriages have run out of exhilaration and joy. Consider how the wine of God's Holy Spirit has been turned into the insipid water of man's speculative thinking. We have attempted to structure our home life and our church life on the basis of what man has to say about heaven (optimistic humanism) instead of what heaven has to say about man. We move forward on man-made premises rather than prophetic revelations.

All the while things were running down at the wedding feast, Jesus stood by. He was guest but not governor. Then came the word of Mary: "Whatsoever he saith unto you do it!" In other words, respect the authority of God's Word. And when they allowed Jesus to be governor a miracle happened.

The prophet introduces God's authoritative Word back into the life of the church and exciting things begin to happen. Our people know that there is a lot of religious activity today, but they haven't the slightest idea where God is significantly moving or what relation he has to it all.

We must penetrate our contemporary religious fanfare today with a word from God. Like Ahab's four hundred domesticated prophets we have lost our grip on the everlasting certainties of our gospel. Those false prophets in

Ahab's court had not heard from the Lord so they just gave the consensus of public opinion. C. S. Lewis once said: "Most political sermons teach the congregation nothing except what newspapers are taken at the rectory" (*God in the Dock*).

After we have received our best training and read our favorite periodicals and genuflected before our institutional systems, what authentic Word have we from the Lord? One shudders to think of what might have happened to Paul's prophetic insight if he had gone to the meeting of the Jerusalem council instead of entering the desert to lay hold upon the Word of God. But since he did, he was free; nobody owned him. And he came back with a Word from God that has guided two thousand years of church history.

III. ". . . and some, evangelists." The gift of the evangelist is one of God's top priority gifts to his Body. He is the bearer of the good news of redemption and release. It is the evangelist who penetrates the social order and makes Jesus Christ a live option among men.

When I hear of those who tell us the day of evangelism is over I think of the comment a friend made about a certain restaurant in our city, "Nobody ever goes there anymore," he says, "It's too crowded!"

Though evangelism may be viewed by some as obsolescent, socially irrelevant and religiously archaic, that is not heaven's point of view. We are witnessing a neo-Protestant ecumenism give way to house-cells, lay witness missions, campus crusades, youth conference, *et al.*, where the Evangel is elevated and thousands are confronting the evangelical faith as a permanently relevant option.

The evangelist will remain a distinctive gift so long as the church is true to its high calling.

Evangelism is the whole work of the whole church for the whole of the age. It is a distinctive thrust. Unfortunately, in some circles it has become a kind of ecclesiastical omnibus, and everybody rides it. One church leader has said, "Everything the church does is evangelism." Bishop Leslie Newbigin tells of a missionary who speaks of evangelism but when asked what he means talks of breeding improved strains of pigs and poultry. William E. Sangster commented: "When we say everything the church does is evangelism, we are close to saying that nothing is evangelism." It is nothing if it lacks character and focus. It can be ever so diverse in its methodology and approach. But it must be definite in its motivation and aim.

Let Sangster define the person and work of the evangelist for us: "Evangelism . . . is that sheer work of the herald who goes in the name of the King to the people who either openly or by their indifference, deny their allegiance to their rightful Lord. He blows the trumpet and demands to be heard. He tells the people in plain words the melting clemency of their offended King and the things which belong to their peace."

Evangelism is not some department of the church, not something self-constituted, not some program or some denominational emphasis. It is the urgency of the soul set afire with the passion of Christ.

Oft when the word is on me to deliver
Lifts the illusion and the truth lies bare;
Desert or throng, the city or the river,
Melts in a lucid paradise of air, —

Only like souls I see the folk thereunder,
Bound who should conquer, slaves who should be kings,
Hearing their one hope with an empty wonder,
Sadly contented in a show of things.

Then with a rush the intolerable craving
Shivers through me like a trumpet-call, —
Oh, to save these, to perish for their saving,
Die for their life, be offered for them all! (Frederic W. H. Myer)

We are evangelists because we are under authority. We cannot deny the grace and joy and illumination of our own souls.

> My heart is full of Christ
> And longs its glorious Master to declare;
> My ready tongue makes haste to sing
> The glories of my God and King!   (Charles Wesley)

We are evangelists because we have come to understand the eternal dimension of the gospel proposition. The blood of Christ speaks more eloquently than ten thousand sermons that this is a desperate mission on which the church is sent. It is not to brighten up a dark world and make life a bit more palatable for men. It is to rescue men from an awesome lostness. Men are made for heaven but are experiencing hell on the inside; made for fulfillment but finding only frustration; made for mastery but are in slavery to themselves; made for safety in God's fold but are an endangered species. Lost souls! This lostness is not necessarily badness as men count badness. It is "awayness." The prodigal was away from home. The sheep was away from the tender Shepherd's care. The coin was away, out of circulation, unused for its intended purpose. That's it! Men are not only lost in crime (treason against just and proper government) but lost to purpose (the vocation to which they are called).

A friend called my attention to a book review in the New York Times which read: "The constant pre-occupation of the characters [of the novel] with the petty and frivolous pursuits make us feel that downright insanity would be an intellectual promotion for them." Not necessarily evil and malicious things but petty and trivial things.

Made for mastery, man is in bondage to vicious human impulses; he is a traitor to his own best self, tainted with low ideals and shabby motives, and untrue to the ideal that slumbers in his breast and comes up with condemning force to shadow all his pleasures. Both psychologically and evangelically men must have the old image shattered and a new image regained. And out of that experience must emerge a total commitment to Jesus Christ and to a Kingdom which is not meat and drink but righteousness and peace and joy in the Holy Spirit.

A highly honored but now deceased missionary friend was at the Jerusalem Conference when William E. Hocking, the Harvard philosopher, gave a public address in which he declared that man could bring himself up to a certain place but would then find that he had not the resources to complete himself. "He must be completed from without, by something beyond himself," said Dr. Hocking. E. Stanley Jones remarked, "I held my breath, waiting to see whether he would say the word. But he didn't. At the close I said, 'Dr. Hocking, why didn't you say the word?' 'What word?' he asked. Dr. Jones replied, "When you said man hasn't enough resources to complete himself, but must be completed by something inside himself, why didn't you say, 'Conversion, New Birth, born from above?'" He thoughtfully replied, "I'm a philosopher, I can't say the word; you are a missionary and an evangelist, you can say the word." "But," Dr. Jones shot back, "I'm not willing for you to turn it over to me; if you see it, you should say it."

We are evangelists because we are debtors to every man in the involvement of human fellowship which demands that what we have seen we must share. This is not mandatory or voluntary, it is inevitable.

> What we have felt and seen,
>   With confidence we tell;
> And publish to the sons of men
>   The signs infallible.

Until this priority is restored in the church, all our planned proficiency is simply shadow boxing. The unity of the church cannot be fully achieved until we are gripped with the necessity of saying it. The "it" that we are to say is further refined for us by the late Archbishop William Temple in this lucid statement, slightly modified by the Presbyterian Church U.S.A., and subsequently used in their New Life Movement: "Evangelism is the presenting of Jesus Christ, so that, by the power of the Holy Spirit men will come to put their trust in God through Him, to receive Him as the Savior from the guilt and power of sin, to follow Him in the fellowship of the church and the vocations of the common life."

That definition gets at the root of our concept of evangelism. It is the "presenting of Jesus Christ"—not presenting the church, though the church is there; not the social application of the gospel, though that is implied; not theology, though that is incipient. But evangelism is the presenting of Jesus Christ. It is that Word upon the heart and out through the lips of the congregation that constitutes this priority for the church. It is true that this cannot be limited to words. As Isaac Watts said: "Words are too poor to set my Savior forth." But telling will never be effective without the words being intelligently articulated. No man's life is so good that by itself it will say everything that is needful to be spoken. Our lives are not that perfect. Our expressions of love and sanctity are too alloyed with base motives and faulty motivation to bring men to a certain verdict about Christ.

Jesus Christ is the one who has a mandate from the Father to evangelize the world. When he is enthroned as our exalted Head, he will send us forth evangelists.

IV. ". . . and some, pastors and teachers." It is here that we need a clear exposition. "And he gave some, apostles; and some, prophets; and some, evangelists; and some, pastors and teachers; for the perfecting of the saints, for the work of the ministry, for the edifying of the body of Christ" (Eph. 4:11-12).

We have mistakenly conceived the pastor of the local church to function as: (1) doing the work of the ministry (2) perfecting the saints (3) edifying the Body of Christ.

But, in point of fact, there is only one function of the pastor. That is the edifying of the body of Christ. There is no comma in the Greek as we read the twelfth verse of Ephesians 4. The pastor-teacher is given "for the perfecting of the saints [that they might function], for the work of the ministry, for the edifying of the body of Christ."

Sören Kierkegaard, the Danish philosopher, has pointed out a misconception in our thinking about the role of the minister and layman. He stated that we had come to think of the ministry as a drama in which the minister or pastor is the chief performer. It is somewhat like a stage set on Sunday morning. The drama unfolds. The preacher is the actor on the stage. God is the prompter behind the scene, feeding the pastor his lines. And the congregation sits as spectators.

Kierkegaard pointed out the incongruity of this thinking. For in reality the people are the actors. God is the audience. The preacher or pastor is the prompter feeding the people their lines.

"The minister," said the late Archbishop William Temple, "stands for the things of God before the congregation, while the congregation stands for the things of God before the world."

The pastor is sent to equip the people. It may be true that the pastor-teacher is not meant to be hyphenated since it is conceivable that there might be two distinct functions. However, they are linked by the same article in the Greek, and the phrase describes what is undoubtedly the ministry of the local church. The first three categories of apostles, prophets, evangelists belong to the universal church. Apostles and prophets were used to establish the church. Prophets were sent with that particular Word of the Lord to activate the conscience, galvanize the will, and direct the ongoing of the church. But the pastor must feed the flock the milk and meat of the Word, and watch over the souls of men as a faithful under-shepherd.

What a high calling is the pastor-teacher ordination. It is the pastor who so often receives the secrets of men's hearts when they open unto him as they would do to no other living soul. He is charged with the responsibility of facing his people with the shame of their sin and then rejoicing with them as those same sins drop into the abyss of Calvary's forgiveness. He comes to know the private ambitions of their souls and is called to stand with them through all the vicissitudes of life, through their failure and success, joy and sorrow, life and death. He shepherds them in the richness of their faith. He teaches them to lift up holy hands in prayer without wrath or doubting. He interprets for them the problems of providence, offers them a comradeship of understanding, supports their human spirit with the tongue of one learned in the things of God. He is diligent to counter their despair, alienation and spiritual sterility. He must help his people weigh their ideas, not only against our age, but against the past. It is here that the unlearned are defenseless, for we are rooted in a temporal provincialism. Our leisure and reading are confined almost totally to the products of contemporary writers, film-makers and television pundits; to what Shakespeare called "this ignorant present." The pastor leads his people in the renewing of the mind by exposing them to the best thoughts of the ages, training them to think God's thoughts after Him.

We need a new assessment of the strategic importance of the pastor-teacher. There are those who doubtless think that a pastor is one who stays "hermeneutically sealed" all week only to "pop out" on Sunday and say his little piece. But the pastor is busy wrestling with ideas, dispensing charities, and championing righteousness all week. One pastor put it: "I don't get paid for preaching, I get paid for what I have to put up with between Sundays."

It is this exercise between Sundays that gives a touch of realism to the ministry on the Lord's Day and keeps the pastor from being ensconced in the pulpit "six feet above contradiction" and out of the range of the feelings and infirmities of his people.

The pastor knows the truth of God's Word. But he also knows the hearts of God's people. He must be firmly in touch with Scripture, fondly in touch with people and flexibly in touch with the Holy Spirit. For example, a pastor who knows the truth must insist on a personal encounter with Jesus Christ, without which man is lost—lost to God, lost to himself, lost to the expanding delights of eternity. And yet there are times when the objective truth of the Word will have to be subjectively ministered to those whom he loves. He must speak "of edification, exhortation and comfort" (I Cor. 14:3).

There comes to my mind an extraordinary counsel from the ministry of Helmut Thielike, which serves to illustrate the delicate fusing of the office of teacher and pastor.

The son of one of Thielike's parishioners committed suicide. With edifying and comforting ministry he came to her with this counsel:

Your son's destiny is an anxiety that troubles your heart. This I can understand, for I too loved him and sought him. And it grieves me that I cannot simply write and say that God loves those whose lives are unfinished, those who are going through storm and stress and that He therefore most certainly received him into His paradise. For the sake of truth and your love I dare not lie to you. Nevertheless, I commend you to the love of God, which is different from a false assurance. "Cast all your anxieties on him, for he cares about you" (I Peter 5:7 RSV). The question of your son's death is an anxiety for you. So cast it on him! We have the promise that we never cast in vain, but that our anxiety always hits home with Him. He feels the impact of it, He catches it, and He takes it seriously. We do not know how He will deal with it or what He will do with it, or make of it. But we can be utterly sure that it will not fall back to us unchanged so that we will have to go on holding it helplessly in our hands. So let your anxiety rest safely with him.

By way of prayer it will have its effect upon Hans—in a way that is hidden from our speculation. All cares are but material from which God wants to form our faith.

As teacher we must confront men with the irreducible truth of Scripture. But with pastoral love we must keep that truth in the context of human need as well as textual fidelity.

It is the pastor-teacher who stays with his people day by day, ministering the full-orbed gospel in a great range of Christian truth. The Great Commission must not be neglected, but it must not be distorted or attenuated. We are sent into the world not only to win believers, but to make disciples. This means evaluation of the intellectual, social and ethical content of the gospel.

This is the pastor-teacher role. And for full maturity the local church is essential to the believer. The New Testament knows nothing of an apostolic and universal church that has no local expression. G. K. Chesterton once wrote: "Nothing is true that is not local." To use a long familiar phrase of an early church patriarch: "He who will not own the Church as his mother, cannot know God as His Father." That may have negative overtones to some. But we cannot deny that God has set the solitary in the family. We are not converted and then put on a lonely road. We are members of a great family in heaven and earth. God's order is for a strong local church, bound together in the indissoluble amalgamation of love, under the discipline of church polity, marching out from its spiritual armory under the captaincy of the Holy Spirit to capture the hearts of men under every sun, then training them and equipping them for the ministry. D. L. Moody expressed the divine motif of such a ministry when he prayed: "Lord, save the elect and then elect some more!" Such is the prospect of "gathering with Christ." This is exciting business!